*The more you travel, the more you
realize how little you've seen.*

Gunther W. Holtorf

ONE YEAR ON A BIKE

FROM AMSTERDAM TO SINGAPORE

by Martijn Doolaard

gestalten

Preface

I've never been away from home longer than a month. All of my previous trips were more or less planned. I love to spend time in the outdoors, reconnecting with nature without the distractions of daily life. It opens the senses and triggers the mind. Why is it that we can endlessly stare into a campfire without getting bored? Is the pureness of the wilderness always experienced as if for the first time, or does it create a sense of belonging to a place we originally came from? Certainly we are not made for sitting in offices five days a week. Although my work as a designer and filmmaker is mostly done sitting behind a desk, I try to reduce this as much as possible. Life has so much more to offer. Why are the most vivid memories in our lives from vacations and travel? When I open old photo albums at my parents' house, the pictures were almost always taken during a vacation. When we travel, we open up. We learn, we absorb, we get amazed. So why then do people travel so little? Is it for financial reasons? Are we stuck too firmly in our daily routines?

Ever since I quit my job at a design agency in 2010 and started freelancing, I've felt more in control of my own life. I've found I can focus more on the things I find important and manage my own agenda. I started to travel more. I made city trips but went mostly to remote natural areas. My favorite countries in Europe are probably Norway and Iceland. With the traveling came photography. I need to create. It's what drives me in life. Whether it's designing a beer brand, directing a music video, writing music, or shooting stills in nature, photography urges me to reach that mountain top and to capture the sunrise in the most beautiful way and not leave until I've seen the best part of it.

A while ago I was visiting Pulpit Rock in Norway with a friend. It's a giant boulder rising above the Lysefjord with a 600-m drop below it. We were going to spend the night there, and while looking for a place to pitch our tent my friend pointed at a nice spot out of the wind on a flat piece of grass. I said, "No, we're going to sleep right on the edge of the cliff. We're here for the thrill, not for a decent night of sleep." I want to zip open my tent in the morning and rub my eyes with the best view possible. This has always been my criteria when I'm camping out.

Traveling to a destination in a certain time frame is how most people travel. I was wondering what it would be like to leave home without much more than a bike and some camping gear for an unlimited amount of time. No route, no planning, no end goal. Live by the day and travel for the sake of traveling.

A year before this trip I started my blog Espiritu-libre.com to share photos and stories from my adventures. I love to escape the city and discover the beauty of nature in remote landscapes. The most beautiful places are often the hardest to reach, so it becomes a sport to discover them. It gives an extra reason to camp out on the top of a hill or deep in a scenic valley.

When we travel, we open up. We learn, we absorb, we get amazed.

So why on a bike? During previous road trips I saw them pass me by: people on heavily packed bicycles, riding through sun, snow and rain. From the comfort of my car I always thought they were crazy. But after reading an article about two German twin brothers cycling from Berlin to Shanghai, I started dreaming about traveling by bike. It wasn't until October 2014 that I rented a bike during my stay in Barcelona to explore the city. Normally I take public transport and walk a lot in cities abroad, but a bike made exploring so much more flexible. I started to think about the idea of traveling by bicycle. The freedom, the simplicity, the open road. It's not so much the cycling itself that draws me but the bigger picture. Always going forward, never turning back. If we look at our daily lives, we live in circles. We go to work, we come back from work. We go to school during the week and we have quality time during the weekends. We go on vacation and we come back home after a week or two. There is nothing wrong with that, but I needed to break that pattern. A new perspective every day. No circles but a straight line: forward. I wanted to travel slower and see more. A bike would be the perfect vehicle for it. While others would say that traveling faster would bring

you to more destinations, I believed that in between two destinations there are 20 more to explore. I searched the web for the kinds of bikes people use, what sort of bags, lightweight gear, itineraries, etc. After a sleepless night spent reading blogs and travel diaries, there was no turning back. When I returned from Barcelona, I immediately went and bought a Surly Long Haul Trucker.

I bought panniers and camping gear, and after only three weeks I left Amsterdam again for a try-out trip to the Swiss Alps. Winter had just begun. It wasn't that I particularly wanted to cycle in winter; I was just too excited to wait for summer. The goal was to cycle into the mountains until I got stuck in the snow and then go back by train. I didn't get stuck in the snow but made it to the center of the Alps in Andermatt in 16 days. It was an incredibly powerful experience to stand on this high point and look back over the mountains and imagine my home invisible and far away behind the horizon. I was totally sold on the idea of a challenging bicycle trip.

That winter I took on a lot of jobs to build up a travel budget. I didn't tell many people about my plans—only my family and two or three of my best friends. I told my co-workers I wasn't available for the coming months, without telling them the reason why. For me, this trip was about freedom and the unexpected. Not telling people of my plan contributed to that. I didn't want people to ask questions or have expectations. I had a lot of questions myself, but I knew that they would be answered along the way. I asked three friends to meet for a drink. I told them I was going to leave the next day. No farewells, no goodbye party, nothing of the sort. I had said goodbye to my family a week before.

At the Scheepvaartmuseum in Amsterdam I asked a tourist to take a picture of me, which I posted on Facebook, saying that I was going to cycle to China. It seemed a ridiculous idea. People reacted both excitedly and sceptically. What was I going to do in China? I had no idea. I wanted to be on the road, and there was a lot of road between Amsterdam and China.

AMSTERDAM

ARNHEM

PRAGUE (p. 40)

FULDA

ROTHWIND (p. 28)

BUDAPEST

BRATISLAVA

BUCHAREST (p. 58)

VARNA

ISTANBUL (p. 78)

ERZURUM (p. 116)

ASTARA (p. 144)

CHALUS (p. 154)

SIVAS

TABRIZ (p. 134)

CAPPADOCIA (p. 98)

PAMUKKALE (p. 88)

TUZ GÖLÜ (p. 90)

KONYA

TEHRAN (p. 166)

DAMGHAN (p. 188)

ESFAHAN (p. 172)

*The complete route from Amsterdam to Singapore. Every dot
is one day on the road. Some exceptionally long sections in
Uzbekistan and India are in combination with hitchhiking or
bus/train to meet visa deadlines.*

N

Russia

Kazakhstan

Mongolia

Uzbekistan

TOKTOGUL BISHKEK

TASHKENT

BUKHARA (p. 204)

Kyrgyzstan

TURKMENABAD

OSH (p. 206)

-HAD

Tajikistan

SAMARKAND

SARY TASH (p. 210)

SERAKHS (p. 200)

Afghanistan

Tibet

China

North Korea

Yellow Sea

South Korea

Pakistan

NEW DELHI

Nepal

DARJEELING (p. 275)

Bhutan GUWAHATI

East China Sea

India

SILIGURI

Bangladesh

TAMU

MANDALAY (p. 304)

MOREH (p. 286)

Taiwan

Myanmar
(Burma)

MONYWA (p. 294)

HYDERABAD

KOLKATA (p. 262)

BAGAN (p. 306)

INLE LAKE (p. 318)

Laos

PURI (p. 258)

GOA (p. 236) PANAJI

MAE SOT (p. 332)

VISAKHAPATNAM

YANGON

Thailand

South China Sea

HPA-AN

Vietnam

VASCO DA GAMA HAMPI

BANGKOK (p. 334)

Philippines

Bay of Bengal

Cambodia

CHA-AM (p. 336)

Arabian Sea

Andaman Sea

Gulf of Thailand

Sri Lanka

PHUKET (p. 330) KRABI

KOH ADANG (p. 348)

KOH LIPE

Malaysia

KUALA LUMPUR (p. 356)

Malaysia

Maldives

Singapore

SINGAPORE (p. 358)

Sumatra

Indonesia

Java Sea

Java

Bali

Banda Sea

Timor Sea

This is everything I owned for the majority of the trip, except for some winter gear, which had already been sent back home when the picture was taken. I bought the guitar in India later in the journey, so it wasn't with me the whole time.

Surly Long Haul Trucker

The bike

In Amsterdam I always rode a squeaky old thing to get around town. Bikes often get stolen in the city so I never felt the urge to invest in a decent one. I'm not a professional cyclist, so I didn't own any proper equipment. But when the idea of long days on the road was planted in my mind, I knew I wanted to go for the best.

So what is the best bike for the job? It is hard to say because a trip like mine covers all kinds of terrain, ranging from rocky surfaces to smooth tarmac. I needed a bike with a simple setup that would be strong enough to carry the heavy load I traveled with. I decided on an iron frame that was easy to weld, with not too many fancy features, so if something did break, I would be able to have it fixed at a local mechanic's. I tried a couple of bikes that were widely recommended for long distances and made by Koga and Santos—brands that make some of the strongest touring bikes in the Netherlands. The features were great, but I didn't like how the bikes looked. When I grasped the handlebar of the Surly Long Haul Trucker for the first time, I immediately fell for it. There's a certain classic feel to the bike, which is made by a Canadian brand. It's a timeless design that has all the necessities required for a long journey yet at the same time keeps things simple.

The only thing I didn't like were the brake switches placed on the tips of the handlebar. This gives the bike a nice retro look but is totally impractical. I replaced the original handlebar with a straight one so I didn't have to take my hands off the steering to change gears. Bar ends and a triathlon steer were added to create multiple sitting positions.

I looked into a way to charge my phone while cycling. I use it for maps, music, and photos so it's an important tool. I discovered a USB hub called The Plug. Basically it is nothing more than a metal USB hub attached to the top of the head tube. In my case it gets powered by a Schmidt Son 28 hub on the front wheel. My phone is attached to the handlebar with a Quadlock case. This was the cleanest option I could find without having too much wiring and extra batteries attached to the bike. However, it charges slowly and the speed needs to be above 13 km/h to gain enough power. I looked into options that involved solar panels, but they all required too much extra gear and wiring on the bike. I also bought four Ortlieb panniers, an Ortlieb dry-sack, a handbag that fit exactly over the front-bars, three bottle-holders, a pump, a little mirror, a speedometer, fenders, and a double stand from the local hardware store. I was good to go.

At Tuz Gölü (Salt Lake), Turkey

Gear

I needed to be 100% independent so that I could spend the night and prepare food anywhere from desert to alpine areas. I already owned a lot of camping gear, but nothing was really small or lightweight enough to fit on the back of the bike. It takes a lot of time and research to find the right gear.

I didn't save too much weight on electronics. For photos and video, I carried a Panasonic GH4 camera with four lenses. Photography was an important part of the journey and I wanted to be able to have all the different focal lengths available in order to get the shot I was aiming for. Both the camera and its lenses are relatively lightweight. An equivalent full-frame camera would probably be double the weight and size, if not more. To process my photos and write my blog, I took my 15-inch MacBook Pro. This, together with batteries, chargers,

hard disks, was the heaviest thing I took. For navigation, I used my iPhone. I used Google Maps when there was 3G and Maps.me when I was offline. There are a lot of expensive GPS devices on the market, but in my opinion, a smartphone does the job in the most modern and intuitive way.

For clothing, I carried a small selection of casual sports-wear. Apart from padded bike-shorts, I didn't buy any typical cycling outfit because I didn't want to look like a cyclist when I was off the bike. When I stayed in a city a bit longer, I bought new clothes that I later gave away. I simply couldn't carry that much. The majority of the trip was in warm weather, except for the high altitudes in Kyrgyzstan, where I bought extra winter gear to survive the cold. Including my food supply, the bike exceeded 60 kg at that point.

BIKE & ACCESSORIES

Surly Long Haul Trucker 28" touring bicycle
Brooks Flyer Special saddle
Brooks hand grips
Ortlieb back roller Classic panniers
Ortlieb front roller Classic panniers
Fjällräven Greenland briefcase
Vaude handbag
Repair kit and spare parts (tools, brake cables,
chain, lubricant, and brake blocks)
Leatherman Wingman multi-tool

CAMPING

Akto Hilleberg Desert tent
Thermarest Trail Pro camping mattress
Mammut Ajungilak Kompakt sleeping bag
Fleece sleeping-bag liner
Cocoon Air-Core travel pillow
Ticket To The Moon tarp (mainly used as ground sheet)
Optimus Nova stove
Quechua cooking set
500 ml Stanley thermos bottle
Quechua Aluminium cup
Mini-sized salt, pepper, sugar, and soap
Tactikka headlamp
Bialetti 1-cup moka pot
Zippo lighter
Buck Cocobolo knife
Sog Tactical Tomahawk
Toiletry bag
Quechua travel towel
Emergency kit

CLOTHING

1x B'twin bike shorts
2x B'twin synthetic long-sleeve tops
1x Nike fleece jumper
1x long thermal underwear
1x Haglöf Rando Flex trousers
Fjällräven Skogsö jacket
Buff headband
Palladium boots
Red Fox gloves (Kyrgyzstan only)
Red Fox snow jacket (Kyrgyzstan only)

ELECTRONICS

iPhone 6
Sennheiser headphones
15-inch retina MacBook Pro
Kindle E-reader
Panasonic Lumix GH4 camera
Lumix 7-14 mm f4 lens
Voigtlander 25 mm f0.95 lens
Voigtlander 42.5 mm f0.95 lens
Lumix 35-100 mm f2.8 lens
Manfrotto tripod + ball head
Spare batteries + charger
Hama ND filters
GoPro Hero 3 camera
GoPro Flex Clamp
64 and 32 GB SD memory cards

EUROPE

DAY 1 - 0 KM

Goals

One week I've been on the road now. Things are going well. Spring is around the corner, the fields are green, and I haven't seen a drop of rain. I ride about 80 km a day. The bike is rolling steadily and my legs are doing a fine job. There are no major pains apart from a little itch in my right knee. When I look at myself in the reflection of a window, I still see a bit of a beer belly. I can't say I'm in great shape, but I have plenty of time to work on that.

I spend most of the day in the saddle. Around 6 p.m. I look for a camping spot in the nearby woods. I make a fire, prepare some food, and watch the stars. I realize this is what I'll be doing for quite a long time to come. It's a carefree life. Which is funny because traveling often brings a lot of hassle. Itineraries, luggage, planning. I'm not really worrying about things because my approach is so simple. It's just me and the bike going east-ward. My mind is clear and my head is full of dreams. Dreams about the unknown, the road ahead, new horizons.

The Netherlands and the first part of Germany are very flat and things go fairly easily, but after about 700 km I encounter the first hills and it quickly gets tough. My legs are not used to climbing. It's the first time I realize how heavy the bike is. At this point I have over 50 kg under my saddle, which is a lot when you consider people ride the Tour the France on a 7- kg race bike. After a couple of days of pedaling up and down I'm exhausted. I'm getting angry at myself for what I've set myself up to do. I'm getting angry at road planners. Why can't they choose a smoother way? Why go up and down? Silly questions, of course. When you travel by car, you hardly sense elevation. On a bike you feel every subtle difference. I cycle half the distance I normally do in a day which feels disappointing.

At the same time, I'm starting to get bored with the scenery. There isn't much change. It looks the same every day. It's all endless German hills. I look at the map on my phone and see the distance I covered. It feels like a lot, but when I zoom out and look at China, I marvel at the distance. This is a joke. What was I thinking? To buy a nice bike and cycle to China? It's insane! I'm losing focus and I book a hotel after a very short day of cycling. I need a break.

It's not about getting to China. It's about everything in between.

Progress is slow, very slow. Looking at the big map is frustrating. I'm too focused on the unknown world ahead. Countries like Turkey and Iran, where the "real adventure" is. Europe feels familiar in a lot of ways. I need to remind myself to live one day at a time. Take tiny steps. Enjoy the details. Be in the moment. It's not about getting to China; it's about spending time in Germany. After about ten days I'll be in the Czech Republic, and I have to make something of that too. If I just keep pedaling, things will come to me. This way of thinking is the only approach that softens the pressure of the enormous distance still before me. To live by the day, take it piece by piece. Absorb the surround-ings and find beauty in small things. The last days are a blur of memories of German country life. Peaceful, quiet villages with characteristic German houses and green meadows. Old folks staring at me from their yards like I arrived from Mars.

If I just keep pedaling,
things will come to me.

Wild imagination

It's the first time I cycle on in the evening. It's extremely dark. Road 289 towards Kulmbach is completely covered in fog. The River Main runs more or less along the road in a few hundred meters on the right, so I decide to find a camp spot along the river; however, there is a railroad between me and the river, and because of maintenance, all the crossings are closed. After a while I find an open crossing and cycle down towards the river. I can hardly see anything because of the fog, but Google Maps on my phone shows me I'm close (a few hours ago I downloaded some satellite information at a gas station). After a while the fog clears up a bit and I see the river. My heart is pounding with excitement. The landscape is beautiful but haunting. That night, lying awake in my tent, I hear more insects and animals around me than ever before.

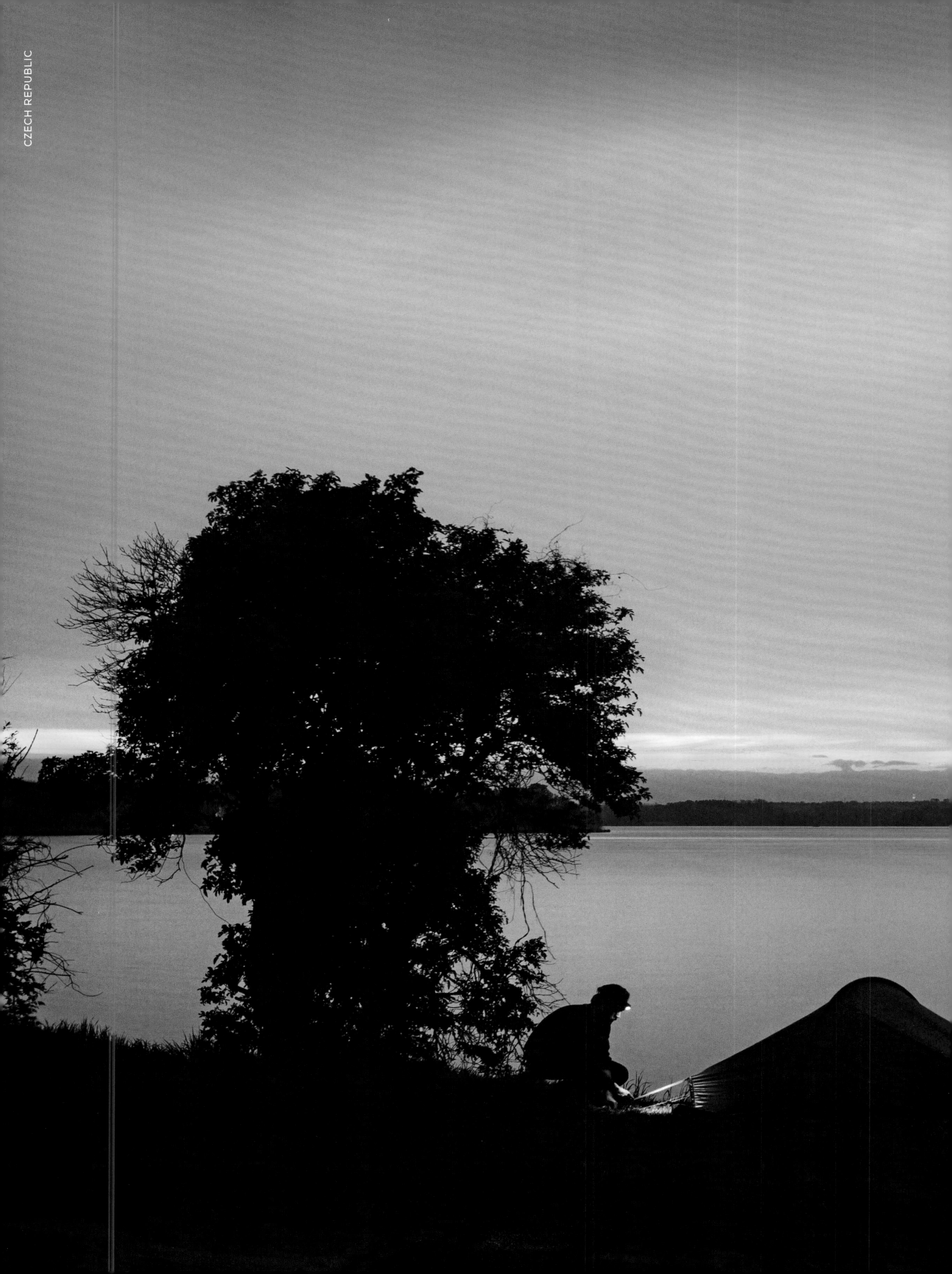

Redefining home

One reason I chose cycling was to be out in the open. Day and night. During my child-hood I camped a lot with my family and went out fishing with my brothers. It always felt like an adventure when our dad woke us up in the middle of the night to drive us to our favorite fishing spot, covered in mist, while everybody else was asleep.

I like the idea of spending the night in places you're not supposed to. In countries like the Netherlands, where wild camping is prohibited and every piece of land has its designated use, it's not always easy to find a camping spot. But with the bike this is a lot easier. Nobody can hear you. With a bike, you can be in the middle of the woods without being noticed. At the beginning of this trip I felt a bit displaced and maybe even inse-cure about where I would sleep at night. But now, once I've pitched my tent, home can be anywhere.

Bike lanes

The landscape, vegetation, climate, culture, the people: you see everything gradually change when you're on a bike. You're much more aware of your surroundings than when you travel by car. From the Dutch plains to the German hills, and from organized infra-structure to a more free form of road planning. In the Netherlands there are bike lanes everywhere. Cyclists are expected to remain in those bike lanes. And when you cycle on the highways, people get frustrated.

In Germany you have to choose between bike lanes and roadways. It's often the case that a bike lane stops with a dead end without any warning. A few times this led to unwanted surprises and I had to cycle back to continue my course. Sometimes I ended up on beautiful cycle tracks through the forest, but other times I was riding on mud paths and over steep hilltops when the main roads would have been a far better option. More and more I chose the the roads instead of the bike lanes. German drivers are very polite and considerate. The first time riding on the highway was a bit tricky, but when I got used to it, it was actually fun.

Once I entered the Czech Republic, things got a lot more straightforward. There were basically no bike lanes, period. From that point on, I was regarded either as a motor vehicle or a pedestrian, which gave me a lot of freedom. I could just go where I pleased because no specific traffic rules applied to cyclists. One moment I was cycling on the freeway and the next I was on a busy shopping street. That's the great advantage of being on a bike there. The roads are not so complicated and you don't usually have to wait in heavy traffic.

The countryside of the Czech Republic was peaceful. Tiny villages, an abandoned train wreck here and there, the occasional dead deer in the ditch (I counted five), and the never-ending yellow fields of rapeseed flowers. I rode uphill and downhill, for days on end, until I reached flat land again in Slovakia. Later I will be covering some distance through Austria, but after that, the term "bike lane" is something I will soon forget.

1289 KM JIŘICE

In spring Europe colors yellow through its fields of rapeseed flowers.

Prague

Reaching Prague felt like my first little victory. There I planned to take a few days off to rest after 17 days of pedaling. I stayed in a hotel at Malá Strana—a beautiful old building with a view on the square right next to Saint Nicholas' Church. I needed to run some errands and buy some camera gear. I enjoyed riding a light bike again over Prague's cobblestone streets.

In the evening I met Steven, an old colleague from Amsterdam who now lives in Prague. He gave me some good tips for printing business cards and told me about the best barbershop in town, where I later got a shave, a massage, and free whisky. The city was packed with tourists, which made it difficult to really rest up. Maybe I got too attached to the silence of the countryside. Eventually, I would have to take a few days off because my knees were starting to hurt. But it was not the right time yet. I was restless. I'd seen this part of Europe and the unknown was calling me onwards.

"Gorp" is a trail mix used by hikers. It stands for "good old raisins and peanuts." I had it for breakfast together with some yogurt, or as a snack along the road. Cycling through towns I always looked for markets to supply my mix with fresh nuts, dried fruits, and chocolate. It's healthy and nutritious, it doesn't expire, and it's very tasty.

Back on the road. Prague is now behind me, and I've decided to focus my route on capital cities. Next up will be Budapest, Bratislava, maybe Bucharest. I don't want to think ahead too much, though. I want to live in the present. The big change from normal life is that every day on the bike feels so different from the previous one. Finding another place to sleep every single day, whether it's a hotel or a campsite, takes up energy. The concept of home doesn't exist anymore. You have to create a new home every night. It will be like this for the next few months. I expected it to feel like a really inspiring way of living, and, in a way, it is. It definitely feeds the soul. But it's also a lot to digest. My head is completely filled with all the things I've seen. The tiniest details of the landscapes. How people live. How they are dressed. How they build their houses, decorate their yards, or prepare their meals. My brain is overloaded with images that haven't become memories yet. In the evening it takes a solid hour or two of staring at a quiet lake or into a campfire to process the day's events.

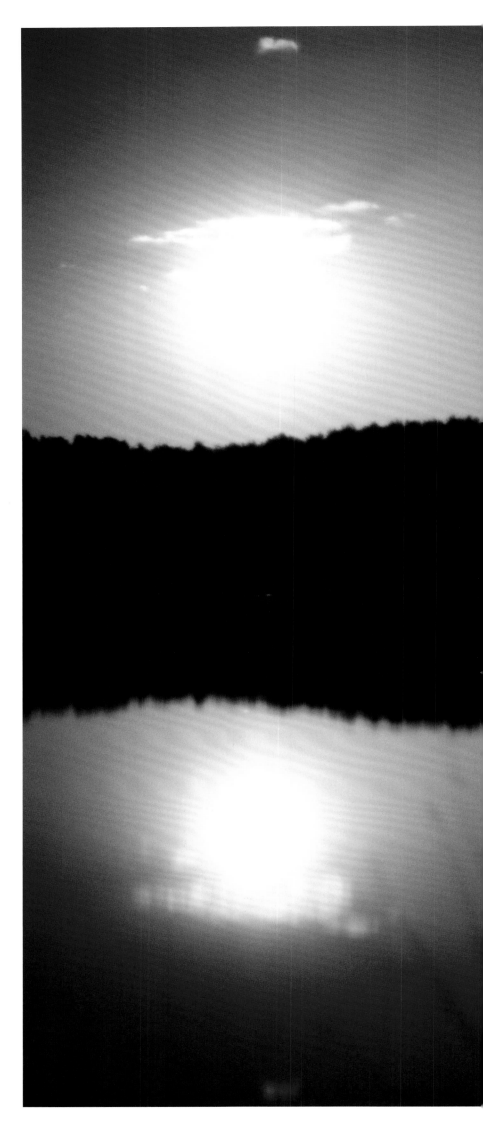

My brain is overloaded with images that haven't become memories yet.

The wild of Eastern Europe

The land gradually gets grittier and more disorganized as I ride east. I am passing through villages where people clear the long grass on their driveways with scythes.

In Romania something new happened. I got chased by dogs. Along a quiet road I was looking for a place to camp. I rode on some dirt roads through the woods, used only by farmers who lived there. In the evening their fences were closed, and when I passed by, the dogs ran along the fence, barking and jumping until I was out of sight. This had happened dozens of times, but I'd never experienced such a level of aggression before. These were monsters. I had the feeling they would eat me alive

if the fence fell over. The next morning I had to cycle back on the same dirt road, and from a distance I saw that a gate in the fence was open. The dogs started running towards me from the back of the house while I pedaled as hard as I could. Because of the sand and pebbles, I couldn't gain any speed. It was like running in a dream. The dogs were barking furiously, while following me very closely till I was far enough from their property. This was the first encounter with dogs and I guessed it wasn't going to be the last. Welcome to Eastern Europe.

Romania was a bigger contrast to Hungary than I expected. You can clearly see the marks left by a period of communism.

Reaching the first town called Arad, I felt like I'd entered a sort of urban jungle. Children were hanging around on the streets, there was rubbish everywhere, and old rattling Ladas with black smoke coming from their exhausts drove past me. Stray dogs roamed wild. Dirty ones that didn't care about anything anymore, including traffic. I found a few dead along the road— hit by cars, guts all over the place. Quite a sight, and a smell.

I'm back on the road again and the people passing give me a lot of moral support. Small Dacias packed with passengers cheer me on and motorcyclists give me the thumbs up. Small gestures like these make it easier to get through the day.

The countryside is more rural than anywhere I've seen until now. Children play with pets and simple toys on the grassy lawns and unpaved roads, or taunt families of geese with sticks. Some old men carry a plough, working the fields. And there are chickens everywhere! It reminds me of my child- hood, when everyone in my street had their own chickens.

So far I've been riding through green valleys. Hungary was very flat. I encountered some hills in Germany and the Czech Republic but nothing major. Soon I will make a hard turn south into the Carpathian Mountains. Things are getting more serious now.

A story about bears

DAY 37 - TRANSBUCEGI - 2627 KM

The forests of Transylvania are residence to the largest population of bears in Europe. I, however, knew very little of that when I entered the Carpathian Mountains.

The Transfăgărășan is a high alpine road that crosses the Carpathian Mountains. Built for military purposes by communist leader Nicolae Ceaușescu in the 80s, it has a forbidding reputation. Hundreds of workers died during construction because of the bad conditions they were forced to work in. Something to think about while cycling over what is now, arguably, one of the most scenic Alpine roads in Europe. Approaching from the north in late May, I was unlucky. In the village at the foot of the mountains, people told me the road was still closed because of the heavy winter snowfall. I had to turn around, which was a bit of a disappointment. I'd been really looking forward to some serious elevation after so many days on flat terrain.

I found out about the Transbucegi, another scenic road starting at Sinaia in the middle of the Carpathians. It starts at about 700 m high and climbs up to 2,000 m. It's a road with a dead end, so it would be a touristy detour on my journey East, but why not? I would need a full day to get to the top, so I planned to spend the night there and enjoy the ride down in the morning.

"You shouldn't camp here! We've had problems with the bears."

The area is a protected national park and there were signs with red crosses prohibiting anything fun. No camping, no open fires, no off-roading. All things I like doing. This probably had to do with the number of bears roaming the area, though. The first section went through the woods and was nothing special, but the higher I got, the more I was treated to breathtaking views over the surrounding woods. A group of people applauded when I approached a viewpoint, sweating heavily and cycling at the speed of a fully packed donkey. After a chat

they left me with the warning not to camp alone. There were two hotels further up in the mountain area, so I thought I'd heed their advice and stay there for the night. At 1,700 m the tree line ended and revealed an open highland with brown grass and snow on the slopes. Eventually, the paved road changed into a dirt path only suitable for off-road vehicles. A few cars were parked, and I saw hikers returning from the mountain. I began doubting my choice for the safety of the hotel. I tend to listen to local advice if I don't know the area myself. Nonetheless, camping would be much more memorable, and I'd stayed in too many hotels already, so I asked some hikers about the bears. They assured me that the animals wouldn't come beyond the tree line at this high altitude and, with that, my decision was made. I spent the last bit of energy I had carrying all my stuff to the top of the hill and peed a circle around my camp, stupidly assuming that animals take territory marks very seriously.

It was pretty cold at 2,000 m. I had left in the morning with the blazing sun on my back, but now I had to put on all the clothes I owned to keep warm. The views were spectacular when the sky turned to gold, waving the sun goodbye. It was a very quiet night. A gentle breeze made the zippers of my tent tinkle now and then, as if someone was trying to open them. It made me alert, and with the bear stories in the back of my head, it was hard to get some sleep. Seeing the sun crawl up behind the mountains at 5.30 in the morning proved to me that I had made the right choice. This was really something special and, luckily, the bears had left me alone that night.

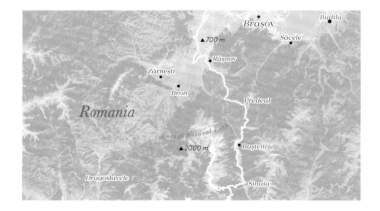

This footprint was close to my camp; it was probably from a large sheepdog.

The Palace of Parliament is the world's second-largest administrative building and was created by former dictator Nicolae Ceauşescu. Built in 1984 (and still unfinished), the building contains over 3,000 rooms and spreads over an area of 330,000 sq m. More than 7 sq km of the historic part of Bucharest had to be demolished for the structure to be built.

Distracted

I stayed in Bucharest for six days. This was much longer than planned because I met a girl who stole all my attention. It's because she had to leave the city that I continued cycling, otherwise my trip might have delayed indefinitely. The strange ways of the heart...

I'm writing this from a deserted gas station on the freeway towards Bulgaria and I'm feeling a bit lost, being thrown back onto the dirty roads. I got attached to the luxuries of the city too much. Bucharest is a city with many faces. While the city houses the remains of Ceaușescu's communist dictatorship, it is also home to some very colorful, inspiring people who illustrate the ambition of a country evolving to become a competitive member of Europe. I was in stores, restaurants, and bars that could easily match the cosmo politan vibe found in NYC, Berlin, or Paris. But not far away in the outskirts, you still face the rubble and poverty that I was getting familiar with from being on the road in Eastern Europe.

Tonight I will be looking for a camp spot again. I need to put my mind to it. Tomorrow I will cross the Danube for the third and last time, heading to Asia. I am not sure what to expect from Bulgaria. While reading travel blogs this morning, I stumbled on some cases of street robbers in the Bulgarian countryside. I can't say it holds me back. It's part of the adventure — just like leaving things behind.

2891 KM - GIURGIU

The Black Sea

DAY 47 – 3057 KM

From the North Sea to the Black Sea. I've reached the end of Europe. It feels like a great accomplishment. The last days through Bulgaria were uneventful and I pushed a little extra so I could take it bit slower going southwards along the coast.

There is something magical in spending the night on an empty beach. When the sun sets, the colors in the sky fade through purple, pink, orange, and green to blue. There is nothing other than the sound of the waves and sand between your toes. Total tranquility. At sunrise I get up, take a swim, and go through my camping ritual with all the care and patience in the world. I put the stove together, make some coffee, write down the distances in my booklet, and read a bit on my Kindle. I have the entire beach to myself and linger till noon, when I get back in the saddle. This is almost too perfect to be true.

Nils

The road is going south along the Black Sea and the beach vibe keeps the speed low. No rush. While I'm oiling my chain at a gas station, I meet Nils, another cyclist with a similar plan—riding east. We have a chat and decide to cycle together for a bit. It's the first time I meet a fellow long-distance bicycle traveler. He's from Bern, Switzerland. There is a lot to talk about. Which route, which gear, visas etc. He built his bike from scratch on a 20-year-old steel frame and updated it with modern parts. He is still using parts of his childhood bike. This makes it a very personal ride.

Nils doesn't use any form of social media—he travels completely off the radar. The simplicity is admirable, although for me it's very important to create and to share my memories from the road. Being able to take photos and tell stories drives and inspires me to do this trip in a certain way. To find special moments and places. Nils is happy with the occasional snap from his phone and sending a few postcards home. This simple way of traveling makes his setup very light. He only has two small panniers on the back of his bike. He sleeps in a bivvy bag instead of a tent, on a mattress so small it only carries his upper body and he wears the same clothes all the time. A choice of reduced weight and simplicity over "luxury" and versatility. Everyone has their own style. His makes him a lot faster. I average about 80 km a day, while he does 130. That's a big difference. I'm used to the idea that faster is better, but for this trip I'd like to think that the slower I go, the more I see and the more I experience.

*The slower I go,
the more I see and
the more I experience.*

TURKEY

DAY 52 – 3327 KM

With a surface area of 1,665 sq km, Tuz Gölü (Turkish for "Salt Lake")
is the second largest lake in Turkey, and the three mines operating
there produce over 60% of the salt consumed in the country. For
the main part of the year, it is very shallow: around 40 cm deep. In
summer the lake dries up, revealing a layer of salt that's on average
30 cm thick in August.

Surprises in Turkey

After the warm serenity of the Black Sea, I left Bulgaria through the low populated hills in the south. It was hot and humid and I was attacked by flies. When I reached the Turkish border, I didn't have enough cash to pay the visa, which was only 25 euros. There were lots of currencies in my wallet, from Singapore dollars to Norwegian kroner, but only Turkish lira or euros were accepted. I got help from a taxi driver who paid my visa and took me to the nearest town with an ATM. I hadn't been in a car for two months, and it felt strange to move so fast over land. Normally it would've taken me half a day's labor to cover this distance through the hills, but it flashed by in minutes. It didn't feel right, but knowing that I made a detour in Romania on the Transbucegi (p. 54) justified the ride.

Turkey was full of surprises. The first night it took some time to find a hotel. I ended up in a bit of a shabby place, but it was better than nothing. Although the sign read "Hotel," the place appeared to be some kind of brothel. At some point a line-up of scarcely dressed girls came out of the elevator. I was sitting in the foyer when they passed, and then I took a seat in the restaurant. The place looked like it was styled for a wedding dinner with tables and chairs dressed up with white linen. In the corner there was a guy behind a keyboard cranking out loud Balkan beats while the room was lit with purple lights. The girls were sitting at tables in the middle of the room. The surrounding tables were occupied by groups of men socializing and waiting for the right moment to step up to a girl to share a room with. I found the whole thing quite fascinating.

I ordered a beer, but after a while I couldn't stand the noise anymore because I was sitting too close to the speakers. When I wanted to leave I got into a bit of a dispute with the waiter who wanted to charge me 40 lira for a beer (12 euros). He had served it with some nuts and cucumber slices that I didn't order and didn't eat. I gave him 20 lira and left for my room. That was the oddest place I'd stayed so far.

On the road the Turkish hospitality is endless. After stepping into a café or restaurant people would often approach me with curious questions and I'd get invited to their tables for free tea and even free meals. Most of the time they hardly spoke English so we'd just sit and drink tea. The basics like name, origin, and occupation were communicated; everyone would know that they had a Dutch cyclist at their table. It was a very social and heart-warming environment and it lifted my spirits during some tough days. The traffic was something I had to get used to. I had to learn that Turkish hospitality is something that's expressed around the table, but on the road it's everyone for themselves. The streets were chaotic, hectic, and loud so I decided to behave in the same way. I shouted, made wild gestures, looked people in the eye, and claimed my space. It seemed to work fine and I enjoyed cycling like a maniac. It wasn't that I was reckless, but you'll get run over if people don't see you.

When I reached Istanbul, it was raining and I rode straight to the Blue Mosque. I asked someone to snap a picture of me and cycled to my apartment in Beyoğlu. I really needed a break.

Swimming in the Bosporus, strolling the narrow alleys of Cihangir, being stared at by stray cats. There's no place like Istanbul.

Istanbul

Reaching Istanbul by bike feels like a great achievement. It's the gateway to Asia and opens up a new chapter of my journey. It's my second visit to this affecting city. The hot sun, the lively shores of the deep-green Bosporus, and the frequent prayers from the mosques echoing through the streets all color the city. With around 14 million citizens, Istanbul ranks in the top ten most populated cities in the world. Infrastructure is chaotic, yet you can relax on one of the ferries where fresh Turkish tea is served or while walking the Galata Bridge, where you'll find a long line of fishermen eager to catch a fresh meal.

I rented a fourth-floor apartment on the east side of Beyoğlu, not far from the Bosporus, with a great view overlooking the old neighborhood. A quiet hideout above the hectic and busy traffic down the hills. I dragged my bike up through a maze of steep alleys with beautifully aged facades, which are occupied by antique stores, coffee places, and exclusive boutiques.

Anca, the girl I met in Bucharest, visited me for a few days in Istanbul. We enjoyed ferry trips, swum in the Bosporus, and strolled the narrow streets. At any time of the day we were welcomed at the "Taxi büfe" around the corner, a tiny restaurant for taxi drivers that we visited daily for some tea or lentil soup. We made up the stories behind the charismatic faces of old Turkish men working the docks or having tea in front of their stores. Not far from our apartment was a little park with a breathtaking view over the Bosporus. Every evening the stairs were filled with people socializing and enjoying the view with a bottle of wine. It seemed as if time was standing still. Istanbul fell over us like a warm blanket, and I let myself fully immerse in it.

Saying goodbye was not easy. I've learned the hard way that a nomadic style of living is as much about connecting as it is about letting go. This trip has been a parade of highlights, and if you live on a cloud, sometimes you fall through. I guess I have to make my peace with that.

The Galata Tower, once named the Tower of Christ in Latin, was built in 1348 at the apex of fortified walls. It was first used to house prisoners of war, later became an observatory, and is now a 360-degree city-viewing gallery.

"In fact no one recognizes the happiest moment of their lives as they are living it. It may well be that, in a moment of joy, one might sincerely believe that they are living that golden instant "now," even having lived such a moment before, but whatever they say, in one part of their hearts they still believe in the certainty of a happier moment to come. Because how could anyone, and particularly anyone who is still young, carry on with the belief that everything could only get worse: If a person is happy enough to think he has reached the happiest moment of his life, he will be hopeful enough to believe his future will be just as beautiful, more so."

———

From "The Museum Of Innocence" by Orhan Pamuk

I've learned the hard way that a nomadic style of living is as much about connecting as it is about letting go.

3599 KM　BANDIRMA

For the last three days I've been cycling the freeways of Turkey, heading south to Pamukkale. With vivid memories of moments in Istanbul with Anca, I have a hard time being back on the road again. More than ever I realize this is a lonely ride. Something I was completely comfortable with before. I need to detach, but I can't handle it and my focus seems lost.

Long days on the road can be hypnotizing. The same repetitive movements for hours on end, broken up only by short stops at gas stations. There is not much to see. For miles I ponder the trash people throw out of their car windows onto the hard shoulder. Old trucks pass me by as I try to avoid the remains of exploded car tires lying shredded to pieces across the emergency lane. It's hot and I'm sporting a thick layer of sweat, dust, and sunscreen oil which stings my eyes. There is the occasional stench of roadkill. Most of the time another stray dog hit by a car. I see the beauty of the landscape but it doesn't seem to move me. I put on some music. It lifts me up and merges with memories from days gone by. I know this will all go away eventually and I need to push on. But right now, I just wish I was somewhere else...

Pamukkale (Turkish for "Cotton Castle") has been made eternally famous by the calcite shelves on the mountain above the village. These are gleaming white, and warm, mineral-rich water flows down over them. Just above the travertines lies Hierapolis, which was once a Roman and Byzantine spa city.

One of the numerous vineyards along the roads in the Denizli region.

Tuz Gölü
A world of white stuff

While examining the map one morning, I discovered a large, white stain exactly in the middle of Turkey. It appeared to me to be the second-largest salt lake in the world, after the Salar de Uyuni in Bolivia. I discovered that because of this lake's size, it doesn't get more than half a meter deep, and after a hot summer it is totally dried out by August/September.

I had to cycle around the lake because there is only one area where the road gets close to it on the northeast side. There is an entry point with a hotel, restaurant, and some tourist shops that sell all kinds of salt-based products. Tour buses and cars stop here to take a break and people go for a walk on the salt beach. About 5 km north of this point I dragged my bike through a barley field so I could cycle on the beach without being disturbed by (other) tourists. After I struggled through some

meters of sticky mud I was standing on a huge plain as white as snow. Depending on the direction of the sun, the surface has a pink glow to it and the reflection of the sun was overwhelmingly bright. The beach consists of sharp crystals on which you'd hurt yourself if you walked with bare feet. The scenery was otherworldly, nothing like any place I have been before. With a knife I carved a bit of salt out to take with me as a memento. Cycling on a flat beach with nothing around felt completely liberating. And again, as in Bulgaria along the Black Sea, I encountered a color spectrum at sunset that I hadn't seen anywhere before.

For the bike this was probably not too great an experience. Salt was in every part. I hosed it off at a gas station, but a day later there was already rust on the chain. I gave it the full oil treatment and hoped the rust problems would be over in the coming weeks.

Fear

One night at Tuz Gölü I had a close call with another pack of dogs. Having cycled through Eastern Europe, this was not the first time—there were lots of stray dogs in Romania, for example. But this time, things didn't go quite so well.

I am staying one night at the hotel on the main road, about 300 m from the only entry point of the salt beach. During the day there are people making stops for sightseeing and walking. In the evening I cycle up the coast to make a time-lapse video of the sunset over the lake. I only take my camera and tripod with me. There is nothing out there but the lake, the freeway, and the mountains. When I return after cycling pretty far up the beach, it's dark. I'd seen some dogs walking around at the entry point earlier, but in Turkey you see stray dogs everywhere. They don't usually bother people, and when you pass by, most of the time they don't even notice. But at night, apparently, different rules apply regarding who owns the beach. About 200 m before I reach the road to the hotel, two dogs approach me. Although it's completely dark, their eyes light up green as a reflection of my head-light. Loudly barking and growling, they slowly approach me.

Over the past few months I've learned a thing or two about encounters with dogs. If you continue to cycle, it means you are running away from them. This makes them think they are stronger so they come after you. Therefore, I usually stop, look them in the eye, and most of the time they back off immediately.

This time I do accordingly, and it seems to work. They back off, until a third dog approaches and then they start circling around me, getting closer and closer. Now there is no way back.

I stand tall and keep eye contact with one, but there is another dog trying to get at me from behind. I start to sweat whilst trying to remain calm. This is getting tricky. In the meantime I extend my tripod while maintaining close eye contact with the dogs. I had dropped my bike in the salt seconds ago to be able to defend myself better. Then I hear a fourth dog barking in the distance and they all walk away.

It looks like I've "won"... I pick up my bike and slowly walk on, thinking the worst is behind me. Still, I'm not quite on the road to the hotel yet. As I get closer to it, more dogs come towards me. I can hardly see them, but their eyes light up from a distance. There are about eight of them; big, dirty, and angry creatures. It doesn't take long before there's a riot starting around me. They are so aggressive that one dog even attacks another. Humans are obviously not allowed here at night. I throw down the bike again and try to scare them off swinging around with my tripod like a maniac, but my behavior causes even more aggression. It's just getting worse and worse, and I don't know what to do. Running means being chased and caught, but it's also not working. I start to shout whilst continuing to try and keep the dogs at a distance. Then suddenly a man approaches with a big flashlight. Slowly the dogs back off. I breathe a sigh of relief. He probably owns one of the tourist shops further ahead, which are closed now.

I'm lucky that there is someone still around. Together we walk to the bike, which is still somewhere on the beach. I try snapping a picture of the situation, but with my heart beating like crazy, I can't find the right settings and later end up with only black pictures. I thank the man and feel that I have never been happier in the safety of a hotel.

I lie in my tent in the middle of an open field. The horizon around me is entirely flat, and although my camp is not higher than 70 cm, I feel exposed. In the distance I hear dogs barking. On one side awaits the now quiet freeway, which is disturbed now and then by a car. I hear a prayer from a mosque: the equivalent of the church bells in Europe. I imagine a man sitting on his knees with a microphone in his hands. It's a distinctive sound. Highly distorted, his rusty voice echoes over the plains. After a few minutes the silence returns. One dog is still barking in the distance. Much further away I hear another mosque broadcasting its prayers. Softer, more muffled. It's the only thing I can hear. My tent is a tiny bubble in a wide no man's land. My heart beats in my chest. What the hell am I doing here? Is this the adventure I was looking for? Sometimes it's too much. I hope the morning will give me answers.

Cappadocia

Every morning throughout the year, about 150 hot air balloons take off from the valley in Cappadocia. It's a scene that makes you forget all the problems in the world for a moment. The valley itself is a unique place, consisting of oddly shaped rocks and numerous caves which people have occupied for ages. I had been looking forward to it as it was said to be one of the most beautiful places in Turkey.

Nils, who I'd met on the road at the Black Sea in Bulgaria, was already there when I arrived. We were cycling totally different routes to the East but had stayed in touch via email. We'd met again in Istanbul and now meet in Cappadocia. After a cup of tea we look for a camping spot in the hills. I'm tired, having cycled 88 km with a headwind and a lot of climbing, so I want to settle for an easy spot next to the main road. But Nils is

persistent in finding a more scenic location and convinces me to climb a bit further up the sandy hills. We end up on a shallow cliff where we set up camp. The sunset doesn't let us down. We dine simply: Turkish bread, tomatoes, cucumber, melon, olives, beer, and Bulgarian vodka. It's nice to catch up and share our experiences from the road. He also passed the salt lake a few days ago but didn't find it very special because it was gray and rainy. This shows me even more that it's the moment that makes an experience unique. Being at a place at the beginning or the end of the day, in rain or sunshine, summer or winter, a good or a bad mood, influences how you perceive a place or a moment. That is why every trip is different.

At 5.30 a.m. I wake up from a bad dream. A thin ray of sunlight pierces through the tent. I open the zipper and when I stick my

head out: instant happiness. The sky is filled with colorful hot air balloons drifting on the wind. The sound of soft eruptions of fire from the balloons is almost Zen-like. What a fabulous thing to look at! I've never been so happy waking up. Nils sticks his head out of his bivvy bag after I shout "Balloons!" They drift

by over the cliff, some coming very close. People wave at us from their baskets.

We're up early. Nils finds some thyme on the edge of the cliff, from which we make tea. Breakfast is simple again, but it tastes good. Fresh melon, Turkish bread, dried cranberries, honey, raisins, and a mix of nuts. After packing the bikes we head for Göreme, a small village in the middle of another fairytale land-scape. We look for a hotel to spend a day off the bike, wash our clothes, and read a bit. It's time to let our minds rest from the long cycling days and the many sights of the past weeks.

Later in the day I start to have a bad stomach. It's the first time on the trip, so I can't complain. We had signed up for a balloon ride that morning, but I had to skip it. In the afternoon I say goodbye to Nils, who is continuing eastward. Maybe we will cross paths again in Iran—who knows? I like him. He's a good lad, or what we would call in Dutch, *een beste vent*. I book a night in a hotel to calm my stomach ache.

99

At 5.30 in the morning I wake up from a bad dream. A thin ray of sunlight pierces through the tent. I open the zipper and when I stick my head out: instant happiness.

A lonely ride

I am sitting on the porch of an abandoned store near a village along the freeway. It's 5.30 in the morning and I just finished my coffee. The last two days I camped under the freeway near a stream. Cappadocia's jaw-dropping scenery feels far behind me as I cover a lot of distance per day. There is not much traffic and the sights are monotonous. For hours I listen to the sound of my own breath as I pedal up and down hills. My back is hurting from the inconsistent headwinds. A gas station appears. I take the exit and ask the operator if there is wi-fi but there isn't. Again. Because it is Ramadan, most restaurants are closed or serve limited meals. I realize how dependent I am on the connection with home, the Western world, Facebook, social media. I feel stupid to admit it, but I really can't do without. I've never felt so far from home.

The next day I'm in a hotel in Sivas. I watch an episode of Mad Men, which makes me feel better somehow. It brings me back to the times I was working in an office during the day and watched an episode on Netflix while having dinner. A simple, pleasant life- with a normal rhythm. It seems a world away. I feel tired and miserable. I miss home; I miss a girl I barely know; I miss steady ground beneath my feet. Excitement and hardship follow each other too fast. I feel like I'm on a roller coaster without brakes.

It's midnight and I can't sleep, but my daily rhythm will get me up at 5 in the morning regardless. I take the elevator down to go for a walk and on the street I see the crowds celebrating Ramadan like it's New Year's Eve. I am surprised by the amount of people hanging out on the pavement, eating ice cream, laughing, shouting. All the stores are open extra hours. I haven't seen this before. Ramadan is different in every corner of Turkey. I sense the joy of these people, but I'm not part of it. I feel isolated and alone. This is a culture far from where I come from. I'm just a passenger, witnessing life lived by others. Tomorrow I'll be going again. And it's like that, day in day out. Am I going too fast? Should I go back? Should I stay longer in one place? These are the questions I'm asking myself all the time. While I'm posting pictures of one adventure, I'm already living the next one. I am having so many great moments on this trip. I have been with such beautiful people. But then they're gone again and I have to leave it all behind.

I need to get myself together.

It takes getting everything you've ever wanted, and then losing it, to know what true freedom is.

—————

From the video for "Ride," Lana del Rey

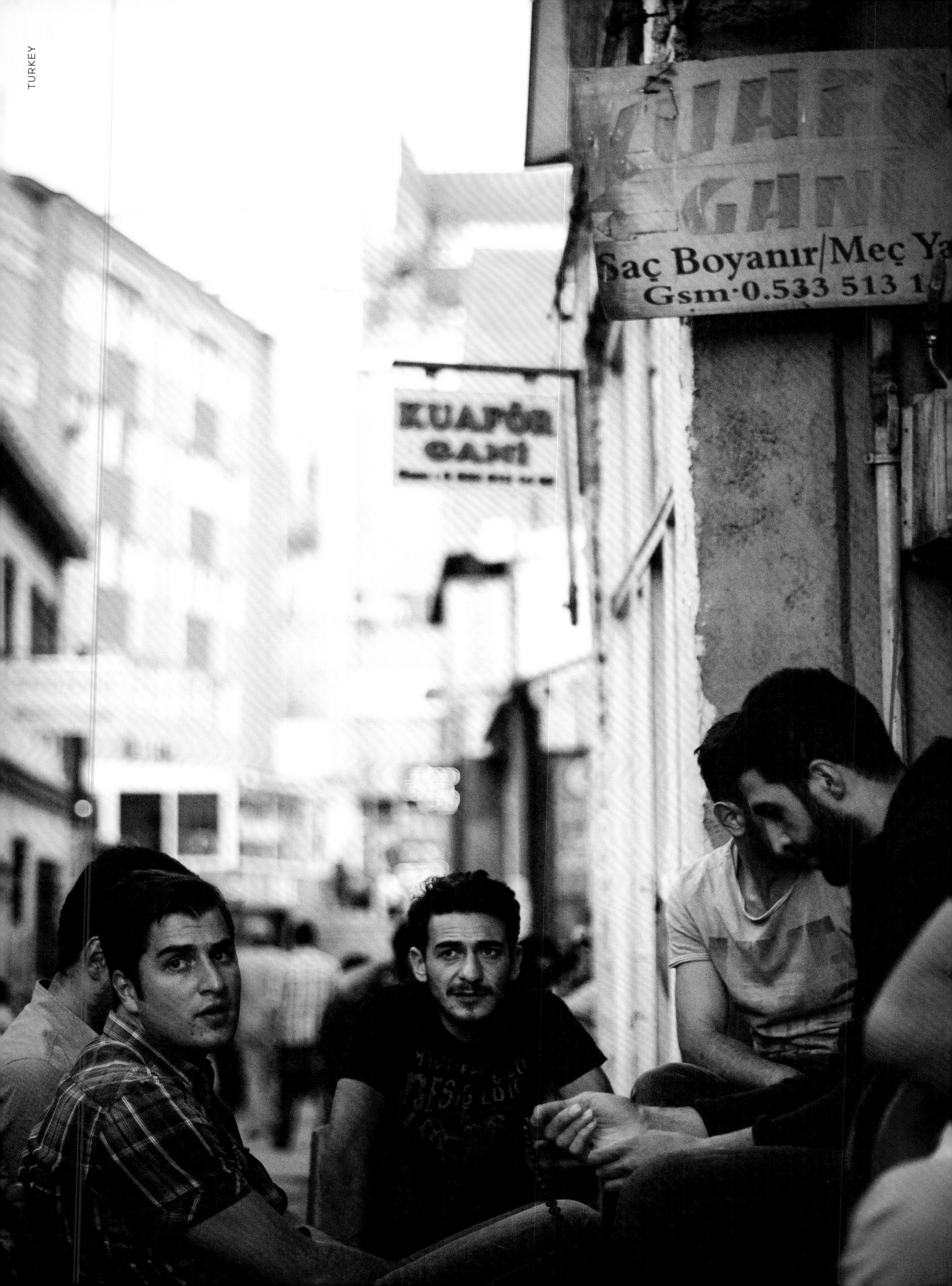
KUAFÖR
Saç Boyanır/Meç Ya
Gsm·0.533 513 1

Turkey
A man's world

I've reached Erzurum, one of the last cities on my route through Turkey, where my visa should be waiting at the Iranian embassy. The process turns out to be drastically delayed. I call the travel agency in London (the Iranian number doesn't respond), who inform me that because of Ramadan, it's going to take extra time. The time it'll take has now effectively been doubled. I'm not going to bore you with the details. Arranging visas in this part of the world takes a lot of effort. I am hassling travel agencies, embassies, and consulates. I left Amsterdam without planning—living by the day and traveling as fast or slowly as I felt like at that moment. From now on, however, I need visas for basically every country I am crossing, which involves careful planning.

So I find myself stuck in Erzurum for a few days. It gives me some time to look back at all the footage I have shot over the past three months and to edit some video material. For the rest of the time I stroll around the city, photograph people, and drink tea with the locals.

When I walk around town, a lot of people stare at me. The smaller Turkish cities barely host foreign tourists and apparently my blonde moustache stands out. People are inviting and open. They are interested in what brings me here. There is a certain warmth to it. European people are generally more reserved, valuing privacy and discretion. Turkey is a man's world, especially in the more conservative regions. Men are very close and affectionate with each other. At first, when these cultural habits were new to me, I found this quite surprising. They hug and kiss, walk arm in arm, sit in cafés with arms over each other's shoulders and it's nothing more than showing good companionship.

When I take a place at an empty table, someone immediately gets up to invite me to his. It's a street full of cafés and there isn't a woman in sight. I'm asked if I want some tea. It's always tea here. In Europe there are different occasions to have tea, coffee, a beer, a whisky. Every moment of the day has its own drink. Here it's black tea all day, every day. One of the guys speaks a bit of English; he is a vet. It's valuable to be welcomed so warmly in such a different culture. There is a "being-one-of-the-boys" vibe, which is stronger due to the absence of women.

Wandering through the streets I search for characterful faces. I like to photograph old men. You can read the depth of their long lives in their faces. Also, they are comfortable posing for a camera. A man at that age usually doesn't mind so much about how he looks in a photo. He knows himself and he is at peace with it. Young people are often more concerned with how they look. They're often insecure and striving for a certain image. The old man (p. 119) I met in a spice store while he was working had this natural grin—a face full of grace and kindness. I asked if I could take his picture and he just nodded. I shot a few pictures while he was trying out a few faces and I saw that he knew that every picture was going to look good. I shook his hand, thanked him, and went on.

IRAN ·

DAY 104 – 5977 KM

Jameh Mosque, Esfahan

At the gates of Persia

A long line of trucks and cars is waiting at the Iranian border. I heard from people that it could take hours or sometimes days to cross the border. I cycle past everyone waiting in the heat and park my bike right in front of the fence, after I've given my passport to one of the guards. While I wait and eat some grapes, people are arguing with another guard about papers. I can't understand what they're saying. It takes about 20 minutes until the gate opens. I proceed underneath a big arch with the faces of the two supreme leaders Ruhollah Khomeini and Ali Khamenei on it. I am excited and a bit nervous.

It's the end of the day. Rolling into the first town, Bazargan, I stop at a hotel, but when I find out there is no wi-fi, I continue. In a store I clumsily try to sort out the thick stack of bills in my hand, which I exchanged in Erzurum. One bottle of water is 10,000 rial. I have no clue how much that is. Do I have enough money for more than a month of traveling in Iran? Europeans are unable to use ATMs or banks so I am carrying a lot of cash for food, accommodation, and visas for the next countries on my route. I enter the next town, Maku. The brownstone architecture set against the sandy mountains makes me feel like I am in a desert town from a western movie. The air is hot and the traffic chaotic.

Even more than in Turkey, people call on me to drink tea or just say hi. "Hello! Mister!" Drivers use their car horns abundantly as they race by with passengers hanging out of the windows. It's overwhelming and tiring at the same time. I need to touch base for a minute. The first day in a new country. I can already remember past ones vividly. I steer away from the road and sit down in the desert. Iran is going to be intense.

Hospitality is important in Iran— even at the roadside.

At the side of the road sits an old man with a little boy. They are eating a watermelon and watch a flock of sheep. When I approach, the man gestures to me to come over. I cross the road, park my bike, and sit down next to him. He points at a watermelon without saying a word. I take a piece and enjoy the intensely sweet taste. It's so hot in Iran, and I am thirsty all the time, no matter how much I drink. We don't really talk. He just keeps pointing at the watermelon to suggest eating more so that's what I do.

In Islam, showing hospitality is of high value, especially if someone travels without company. People tell me that receiving a guest is like receiving God. We sit there for a few minutes watching the sun sink. I take a picture. They smile. Then the watermelon is finished and I go on.

A homemade Iranian meal. Meals are generally served on the floor in Iran.
In this picture, the objects that look like towels are actually bread.

Invite
Lost in translation

I was looking for a grocery store where I could buy some food for breakfast. I cycled to a village near the highway. It was quiet. The standards of living were very basic and simple. Then I came to a store, if you can call it that. It was more like a living room. Inside were three women and the stock on the shelves was very limited. I just needed some bread, eggs, and tomatoes, but the women didn't seem to understand a word of what I was saying. I pointed at a stack of empty egg trays. They had one egg left in the fridge, and it was not for sale.

This is not working, I thought to myself. I really need more resources to explain what I need next time. The language barrier is bigger than expected. If I don't eat properly, I can't cycle these long distances. I am pushing my body to its limits. Last week in Turkey I had a very bad day because I didn't eat enough. My legs lacked any power and felt like two sacks of water. I could barely drag myself up the mountains.

I left the store and outside a guy on a motorbike stopped in front of me. Friendly face, ironed shirt, hair combed with care. I asked if there was another store in the village, explaining that I was going to camp somewhere in the fields. He shook his head—no—and used his hands and feet to explain I could sleep at his place. I thought for two seconds. Why not? In the meantime, the whole village had gathered around my bike. I answered the questions that come to me 20 times a day. "Where you from? Where you go? Why?" Everyone stares at the bike. Some pinch a tire, checking the pressure. Why do people do that? It's the same as kicking the tire of a car with your hands in your pockets. Just strange.

I followed the guy on the motorbike out of the village; his name was Masud. After a while we approached a small farm. There was a dog and a bunch of chickens roaming the yard. Masud calmed the dog when it began growling at the unknown guy on the bike. The house appeared to be a small stone factory owned by Masud's father. There were three other men. They were washing their hands, finishing work.

I got invited into a small living space, which I entered after washing my hands and taking off my shoes. Masud prepared some bread, eggs, and cucumber. Very basic food, served with lots of tea. We all sat on the floor on some pillows and a Persian carpet. It was the first time I sat on a Persian carpet in Persia. Masud's father was the only one who spoke a bit of English so communication was marginal, but I could show photos and

---

"May God be with you."

---

my handwritten track record to show the development of my journey. Another guy, Ali, held up his phone and showed a video of a big dog barking loudly. "My dog!" He smiled proudly. I complimented him on his dog. Then he showed me some pornographic pictures on his phone, probably to show off or start off some kind of bonding. I wondered where the women and children were, but apparently this was a working space where the men occasionally slept. The family lived at home in a village or town nearby. We all sat on the carpet; there were no chairs or tables. I did some work on my laptop. There was no wi-fi, of course. Next to me Masud's father rolled out a cloth and kneeled for his prayers. Later we sat outside in the dark eating melon and smoking cigarettes and had more tea. I asked Masud what his favorite drink was. "Water," he said. Of course—what was I expecting? A single malt on the rocks? I was waiting for the moment they'd bring out some illegal vodka, but it didn't happen. Two months without alcohol. I wanted to go to sleep early to keep my rhythm so I asked where I could pitch my tent. Masud's father insisted that I slept inside but I preferred to sleep outside where it was less hot. I wished the man goodnight. "May God be with you," said Masud's father.

↑ Samira is 24 and lives with her family in a large house in Tabriz.
I was offered a bed and meals for free when I approached her
brother on Warmshowers.org, a hosting website for bicycle
travelers. In Iran most people live with their families until they
get married.
→ An old farmer I met along the road.

6353 KM   KURDKAND

Akbar

This is Akbar from Marand. He makes a "hobby" out of spotting all of the international cyclists coming through Iran. Over the past three years he has met 643 of them. He waits alongside the road and offers them a bed or a meal. He knew I was coming because someone in Turkey had sent him a photo of me when I was cycling through there. When I met him on the road, he asked if I wanted to have lunch at his place. Since this happened quite a few times a day in Iran, I didn't say yes at first, but he was persistent enough to lure me in. As we cycled together through town, people cheered that he'd "caught" another one. He manages a small market store and showed me a guest book displaying all the cyclists he had hosted there. It was carefully categorized by country and featured cyclists of 47 nationalities. Twenty riders were from the Netherlands.

6473 KM SARAB

↑ *Young woman working in a grocery store in Talesh.*
→ *Women-only bus in Ardabil. A lot of public transport
in the bigger towns in Iran is segregated by gender.*

The Caspian Sea

DAY 112 - 6602 KM

The infinity, the stillness, the purity—there is something captivating about waking up at the seaside. After the Black Sea and the Sea of Marmara, the Caspian Sea is my third ocean so far. I remember one of the best moments from this journey up to this point: camping at the Black Sea in Bulgaria roughly two months ago. For seven days I cycle along the Caspian Sea from town to town. It's the part of Iran that's green—a rare quality given that the country is mostly desert.

Astara is the first town at the seaside, right on the border of Azerbaijan. Families crammed into small cars try to find parking spots close to the beach. It's not particularly the beach life I am used to. No bikinis, obviously. It looks like women are not even allowed to swim. Even some men keep their clothes on while swimming. There are no loud beach bars, resort hotels, or anything of that kind. Tourism hardly exists here. It's very sober and modest, like the Iranians are in their style of living.

No beach clubs, no cocktails, no bikinis.

After a quick bite to eat I cycle out of town to find a place to camp. There are people on every beach, driving their cars on the sand and making fires for roasting meat. There are no rules here. It's a happy chaos, and because the weather is so warm, people stay in the water till it's dark. I find a small pier, where I decide to park my bike. It's a perfect camping spot and I assume the few families still on the beach will leave for the night. It's completely dark when I dive into the sea. It's unexpectedly warm and there are almost

no waves. While I float on the smooth water, I look at the stars and memories of some night-time skinny dipping in Rimini come to mind. My ears are under water and I listen to the sound of the sea. This is just perfect.

Back on the beach some people light up a campfire. I have to join them for some watermelon. Around eleven I get in my tent, and in the middle of the night I get unpleasantly awoken by a dog barking and growling right outside. I jump up and think of what to do. While I wait, staying hidden in my tent, the dog continues being aggressive. Is it happening again? I am probably camping on his favourite spot. After a minute he backs off and I heave a sigh of relief. I can't get back to sleep and wait for the sunrise, sitting on a rock, watching the sea. Far out on the silk-smooth water a fisherman drifts in his rubber boat. Other than that, there is nothing else to see. Just me, him, and the mesmerizing gradient of warm colors. There's a thrill in waiting for that moment the sun sprouts up from the horizon like a liquid ball of fire. Later when I prepare breakfast the fisherman comes by and offers me some of his catch. I politely decline but join him for a cup of tea. We sit there for a while, the only ones on the beach enjoying the sunrise. The next mornings will be like this. For 300 km I will cycle east along the coast. Then there will be a hard right turn into the mountains, climbing up the 3,300 m to Tehran. But I don't want to think about that yet.

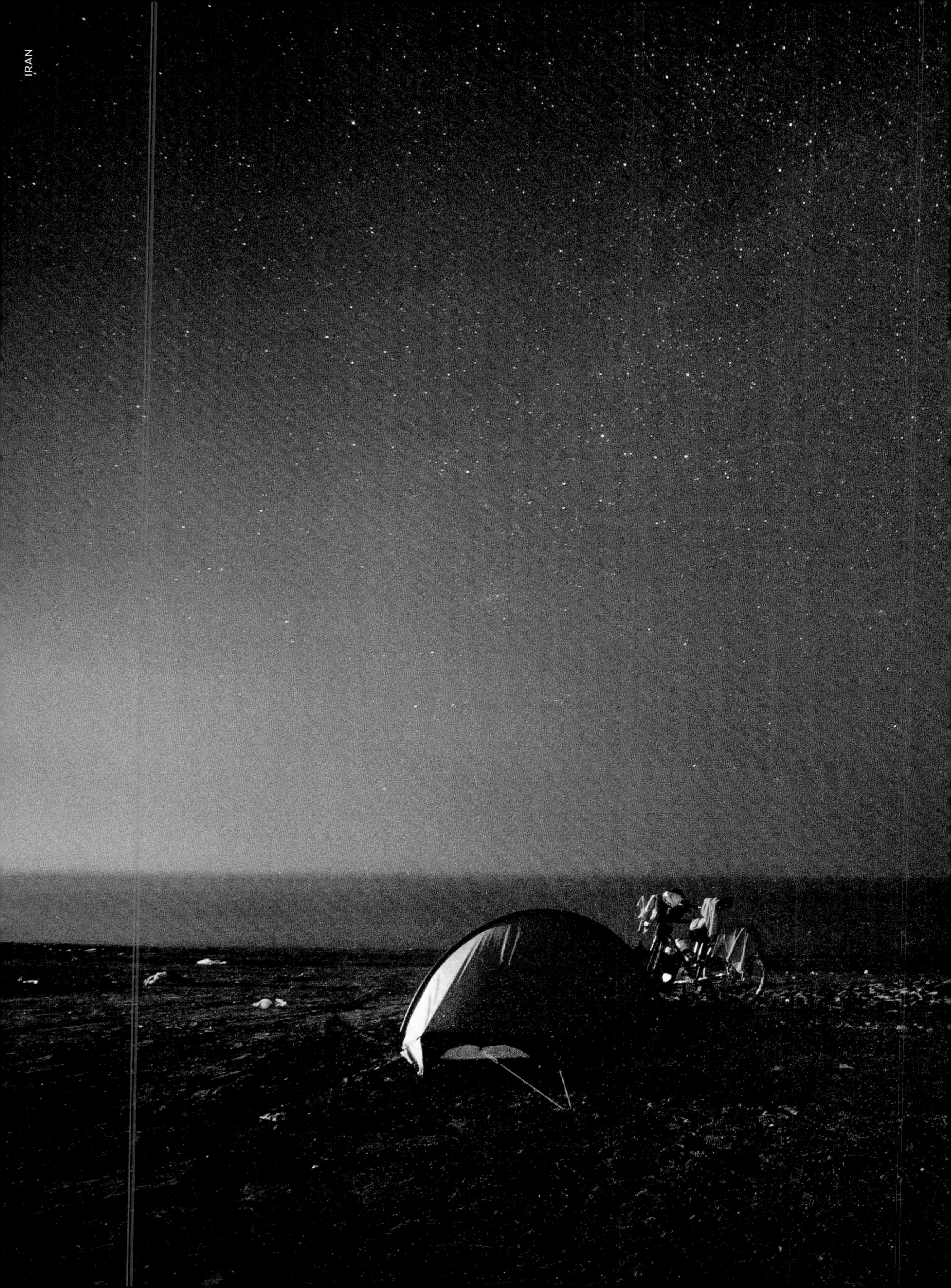

Midnight swimming

I meet Philou and Damian, a Belgian couple, on the road and we cycle together for a day. They are on their way to Uzbekistan on a specially built tandem. It's a fun way to travel as a couple. When looking for a camp spot we end up on a large beach. There is a lot happening. People hang around till late, driving around in rusty cars and on old motorbikes. There's a lot of litter everywhere. Dogs from nowhere wander around and even a cow walks by our camp. The Caspian Sea is actually a lake; it's not salty and the pleasant temperature makes for a perfect midnight swim.

Crawling to Tehran

DAY 117 - 6986 KM

Coming from below sea level at the Caspian Sea, I had to cross the northern mountain range in Iran in order to reach Tehran. The road was busy with a lot of cars escaping from the city to go to holiday destinations at the seaside. With an elevation of 3,300 m, this was the longest climb of the trip.

The mountains symbolize love and hate. It takes me three days to cross the mountain range between the Persian coast and Tehran. The main road climbs from below sea level to 2,700 m altitude, then after a long tunnel it goes down for a few hundred meters, and after that it goes up to the summit at 3,300 m.

It is a holiday in Iran, and a lot of Tehran's citizens are on their way to the seaside, which makes the road very busy. I need to be cautious because there is not much space, but people are in good spirits, cheering from their windows and supporting me like I'm cycling the Tour de France. Regularly there are arms sticking out of windows offering peaches and frozen bottles of water. I expected to be alone on the mountain pass, but I'm far from it. Almost everywhere I stop for a break I get invited for some tea and one time a man even walks up to me to offer a pre-cooked dinner which has been prepared on a stove in the back of his car. Every day, I once again witness how valuable foreigners are for Persians. The man is with his family and I ask if I can take some pictures of his beautiful daughters. They are more than happy to pose, and when I'm done, a lot of selfies are taken with the "hairy stranger" from the West. Many Iranians seem to feel they have to prove themselves to the rest of the world to change their image and so will do their best to make you feel welcome.

> People are in good spirits, cheering from their windows and supporting me like I am cycling the Tour de France.

The third day the road gets steeper, which lowers my average speed to a silly 7 km/h. I take a lot of short breaks and eat twice as much to compensate for the heavy workout. Luckily, my body is doing really well. My mind goes back to the first weeks in Germany when I was dreading ascents of a mere 500 m. Those were nothing compared to the altitudes I'm facing at this point. I know that if I eat properly and keep the right pace, I can rely on my legs.

At the top there is a tunnel, after which the road goes downwards for a few kilometers. Then it splits and I need to make a decision. I can follow the main road down and end up on the west side of Tehran, or I can go east, climbing further up to a height of 3,300 m and ending up on the east side of Tehran. I feel east is where I need to be, so I take a deep breath and make my choice. The road turns out to be even harder than I thought, with no less than 19 hairpin bends and a constant inclination of 12–15%. I become exhausted. At every second bend I need to hold still because my heart is pounding too fast. I'm questioning what I'm doing and I'm close to giving up. This is madness. But at the same time, I realize that if I just take the time, I will make it. After a grueling three hours in which I cover only 6 km, I kiss the sky at the magic 3,300 m. The summit overlooks the entire valley and I take a really, really long break. It was the toughest climb on this trip so far. I was in the saddle from 8 in the morning till 9 in the evening. In the end though, the view alone made it totally worth every minute. And from here on, it's downhill all the way—squeezing the brakes and enjoying the vistas until Tehran's skyline appears on the horizon.

At every second bend I need to hold still because my heart is pounding too fast.

Blue Saipas (Nissan Juniors) can be seen all over Iran. Unbreakable cars that are loved and feared on the road. They are used and abused as working vehicles by farmers and middle-class professionals. No matter how beaten up they get, somehow people seemed to manage to keep them running. Here are some proud owners who offered me a cup of tea.

The Afghan shepherd's boy

DAY 119 - 7102 KM

A great thing about traveling by bicycle is the numerous little surprises you come across on the road. On my way to Tehran I spent a night on this little farm deep in the Alborz Mountains.

We both probably found
each other equally weird.

I still had one day to go to Tehran. Searching for a camp spot was a bit of a challenge because of the steep slopes. I went off the main road onto a dirt track up the mountain. After some time, I came across a young family having dinner in a small field. They were from Tehran but heading for the seaside and asked me to join their picnic.

There was a small shed in the field owned by a shepherd's boy, who was herding his cows. The family told me he was from Afghanistan. They continued their journey. I walked up to him to ask if he was OK with me pitching my tent on his field. He didn't speak English. He actually didn't seem to speak at all, just kept staring at me. Even universal signs like nodding yes or no, thumbs up, or making a triangle tent shape wouldn't elicit a response. I had the feeling I was talking to a statue. After a while, I just guessed he would probably be OK with it and he started to repeat every word I said to him. I parked my bike next to his shed, and while I went through my routine he watched everything silently. There was a water tub in the field where I could wash myself. My shorts and shirt were soaked with sweat after climbing 1,300 m that day so I took everything off and washed myself. The Afghan boy followed every move. He brought me soap from his shed and then he came and stood next to me and patted my butt

a few times, giggling weirdly. I found that a bit weird and tried to explain I didn't feel like being patted on the butt. He was probably surprised that it was so very white. He opened up and became friendlier as the evening progressed. I was offered some tea and melon in his shed. To have some form of communication I let him flick through the photos on my iPhone. He was totally fascinated by it and probably saw a lot of things he had never seen before. This reminded me of a conversation I'd had with a French traveler who had worked for an NGO in Afghanistan. He'd said most farmers there live a simple life without electricity, computers, or the internet. It's hard to imagine what it would be like for them to hold something like an iPhone with the newest technology.

It was a starry night and from the field I could see way beyond the mountains. I took out my camera to shoot some long-exposure images. The Afghan boy was flabbergasted when I took a picture that showed more stars than the human eye could see. After some fun shots in which I made drawings with light and long exposure, I said I was going to sleep. He kept watching me while I got into my tent and stood there for a few minutes after I closed the zippers.

We both probably found each other equally weird.

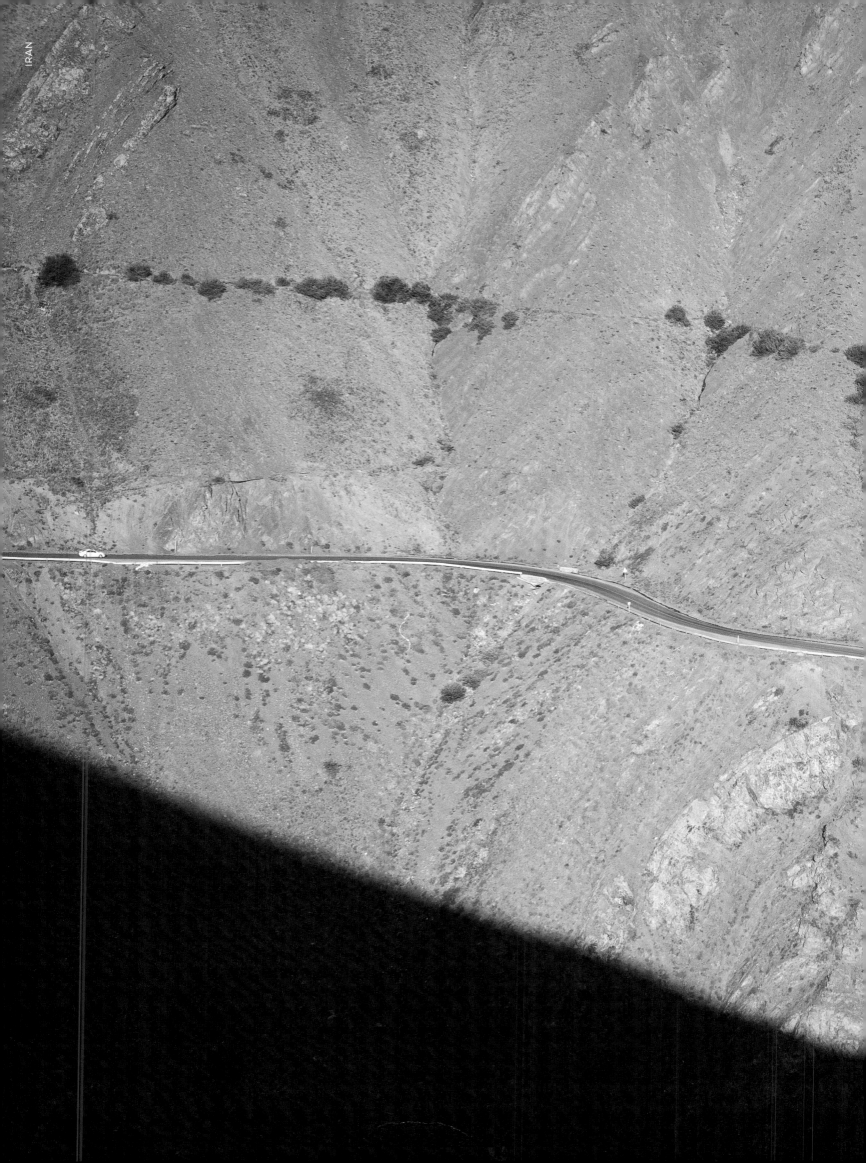

Tehran is the largest city in Iran and it covers over 707 sq km.

Tehran
Bike repairs and visas

In Tehran I stay at different places and one of them is Ali and Mesha's house. It's one big living room where we sleep on the floor surrounded by weird furniture and random stuff. It's also a typical traveler's house—they are both outdoor fanatics who host other travelers and organize trekking tours on Damavand, Iran's highest mountain. I'm not the only cyclist staying there. I meet Anson from China, who has just "done" Africa and currently has 25,000 km on his speedometer, and Ann from Sweden. She is more or less my female counterpart, being a designer, blogger, and world cyclist. She even has the same bike.

We all spend a few days in Tehran to arrange visas for Central Asia. This gives me time to rest and fix my bike. I had some gear shipped in from the Netherlands, thanks to Kaptein Tweewielers. They sent me new tires, brake rubbers, liquids, sidebars, and a new mirror (I lost mine somewhere along the way in Turkey). The drive-train needs a thorough clean, as it's full of grease and dirt. One spoke has given up and there's a dent in the wheel, so Ali drives me on his motorbike to a bike store on the other side

of the city. I carry the wheel on my back and Ann follows on the bike because she needs a new chain.

Arranging visas is the least fun part of this kind of trip. All the embassies are located far out of the city center and Tehran is a nightmare to get around in during the heat of summer. Traffic-wise it's one of the busiest and most chaotic cities in the world. Add to this that most embassies need to be visited twice, opening times are limited, weekends are on Fridays and Tuesdays, and that the online information about application rules changes all the time. You need to get documents printed and make copies of passports. Some embassies want pass-photos in color; others want them in black and white. You need invitation letters from travel agencies and sometimes a recommendation letter from your own embassy. You need to know your entry and exit dates, which border crossings you will take, and so on and so forth. If you deliver one thing too late, the whole process can be delayed for days. The freedom and open borders of Europe lie very far behind me.

Motorcycles are the number one mode of transport in Tehran. Most commonly, people use old Hondas from the 80s. Some designs used are still in production only for Iran. Women are not allowed to drive motorcycles, so you often see whole families, pets included, on one bike.

Esfahan

———

DAY 127 - 7127 KM

Esfahan, a desert city 500 km south of Tehran, is Iran's historical jewel. It's a place where the country's Persian heritage is wonderfully well preserved and a quiet and sacred location that's a world away from the chaos of Tehran. I was happy to relax and explore the city while my visa for Turkmenistan was being processed.

At a flea market in Tehran I bought a traditional white cotton outfit. Partially to have something comfortable and cool to wear under the desert sun, but also to fit in with the culture. Of course, I didn't fit in at all—most Persian men just wear Western clothes. It happened more than once that people referred to me as Jesus. Well, I've always been taught to try and be like him, so that was probably a positive thing. In the heat of the day I walked around the square of the Jameh Mosque, one of the biggest and oldest mosques in Iran. It was noon and hardly anyone was around. I sat there in the shade of the empty square, staring at the calligraphy on the walls and watching the pigeons fly from corner to corner. The architectural detailing seemed endless. It didn't take too long, though, for the hot sun to cover me in sweat. Apparently that's the reason people stay inside at midday.

A young imam walked up to me and asked if I was religious. I answered that I wasn't part of any religion. "Then you cannot be here. You have to be Muslim, or Christian, or of any kind of religion." That didn't make sense to me. I asked him if he thought I was a bad human as I'm not religious. He didn't understand me and asked a colleague for advice. Later I mentioned that my father was a minister in a protestant church and that made everything alright.

Emam
Ali Square

I stroll around the old bazaar at Emam Ali Square looking for a traditional tea kettle. At a Persian carpet store I meet Milad who helps me out in finding one of decent quality. He knows his way in this maze of alleys where you can easily get lost. I love all the detailed artworks, clocks, copper pots, and plates, all decorated with Persian calligraphy. The smell of the rich spices. The sharp sun shining through small openings in the stone arched roofs, illuminating the brown dust particles in the air. Old men working their craft, keeping their stalls clean, and enjoying the social environment of this timeless place.

At the carpet store, Shantia Ghafarian tells me all about his carpets. From the weaving process to the locations where they are made. The way they color the silk, the way they connect the patterns and designs. The stories behind the iconography and patterns are endless. In every house in Iran you will find Persian carpets, from all times and places. You have to dig deep into your wallet to buy one — especially so for those made from silk, which are worth a small fortune.

At night we hang out on the shores of the dried up Zayandeh Rud River. Walking along the old bridges where groups of people sing songs deep into the night. Emam Ali Square is filled with people eating on the grass. A joyful, happy chaos with large families on carpets drinking tea and preparing meals. Children are scattering around; old folks are enjoying a traditional water-smoking pipe in the warm air of the Persian night.

Desert ride

DAY 133 - 7288 KM

A 1,200-km trip through the Dasht-e Kavir Desert from
Tehran to the border of Turkmenistan.

Along the roads in Iran you often find large writing on buildings and mountains. Sometimes people write the names of one of the 12 imams of Shia Islam. You also sometimes find quotes like "Down with the USA." It's government propaganda from the 80s rather than something that is endorsed by the local people. But in this particular case, it says "Mahdi Tools Company." An advertising billboard – Persian style.

The ride is uneventful. Plain land as far as the
eye can see. Black gravel fields alternate with
brown, rocky surfaces. But the nights are magical,
bringing the brightest stars I've ever seen.

The old man and the desert

In the shadow of a traffic sign I find an old man sitting on the side of the road. He has the appearance of a little boy but a face lined by many years. I have no clue what he is doing here or what he is waiting for because there is nothing around for many kilometers. After I try to have a conversation with him, I continue on my way. A few kilometers later I find a man waving at me from out of a digging machine. I pull over and stop to talk to him. It looks like he wants to offer me some tea, but it turns out he is actually asking me for tea. Then the old man I met earlier also joins us, carrying his big back-pack and an empty water bottle. I have no idea what this situation really is, but there are two men in the middle of nowhere without water, so I give them a bit of mine. I have more than enough. It feels like with this small gesture I can give something back to the generous people of Iran who have been so kind to me.

The imperceptible, smooth sound of a perfectly oiled bike rolling over brand new tarmac in the heat of the desert with the wind from behind. The light hum of the tires reading the road. A steady 30 km/h. Two bottles of *yakh* (ice) on the top of my backpack provide me with ice-cold water for the next two hours. After that, the temperature reaches around 40°C. I'm happy to be back on the road. I left Tehran for the serenity and nothingness of the desert and that is exactly what I find here. I continue eastward to Mash-had, the last city I'll visit in Iran.

My new goal is 900 km away. The sights of the desert are simple. After two days the wind turns and comes from the east, which slows the cycling and makes it tough to get ahead. In the far distance I see wild camels for the first time in my life.

I go from city to city. Garmsar, Semnan, Damghan, Sharud, Miami. Beyond those cities my food-and-water management needs more careful planning. It's the first time I am using my 10-liter water bag. This makes the bike significantly heavier. It's hot but that doesn't bother me much; I am used to it now. Messages from home tell me that summer is over in Holland. My little boat almost sunk in the Amsterdam canals because of the heavy rain. I haven't seen rain in weeks. I left home just before spring; this journey seems almost like another lifetime.

When I pass a village, a police officer gestures me to stop. First I think it's because I'm expos-ing too much skin again. The law prescribes long trousers and sleeves till the elbows, but that's too much for me in this heat. The policeman doesn't make any fuss about that, instead he just wants to chat and take a selfie. The law is easier on tourists sometimes. Later I meet Philou and Damian from Belgium again by surprise; we cycled together some days ago in the north of Iran. It was nice catching up, camping under the stars, and sharing stories from the road. The next day they take a more northern route because they have more time on their visas.

Saved

I'm low on food and water when dusk arrives. I need to look for a camp spot, but first I need to eat. But where? And what? There is no gas station or store anywhere. This unplanned thing seems totally wrong in the desert.

At some point I notice houses further up in the hills. I decide to cycle there and seek out the Persian hospitality once more. A dirt road brings me to a yard with a puddle with geese in it. A dog starts barking but appears old and blind so it won't do me any harm. An old man sits on a motorbike talking to a child. I presume he's the farmer. I stop. "As-salaam alaikum," I say. The farmer returns the greeting, and we shake hands. By making a triangle shape with my hands and a sleeping gesture, I explain I'm looking for a place to camp. He seems to understand, and I follow his motorbike around the yard. He shows me a small mud-brick house with a porch, out of the desert winds. Perfect. I pitch my tent and take a shower, which involves warming up a bottle of water and rinsing myself clean.

I cycled around the village, which is not more than a few similar mud-brick houses, and see the farmer sitting in the field herding his sheep. I sit down next to him and show some pictures on my phone. He makes a gesture to his mouth, asking if I want to eat. At the houses his wife prepares me a meal that I can take to my campsite. Spicy eggplant with potatoes and eggs, a bowl of fresh yogurt, green herbs, and "towel" bread—I call it that because it's the thinnest bread I have ever seen. I cook some left-over spaghetti that I found at the bottom of my pannier and enjoy a great meal.

Around 10 at night I crawl into my tent, which I'd placed on the porch to shelter me from the strong winds. Sleep catches me quickly. Suddenly I get woken up by the sound of two cars that stop right in front of the house. Three men talking and laughing in Persian. I thought nobody lived here, but I was wrong. I was camping on someone's doorstep. It must look hilarious to see a bike and a tent blocking your doorway. I stick my sleepy head out of the tent to see what's happening outside. The guys laugh at me first but approach to shake my hand, being as friendly and inviting as ever, even though I've camped right on their doorstep. They even offer me some extra blankets. After they go into the little clay house, I can't get back to sleep so I put on some clothes and go inside to join them. There's fresh melon, crisps, and drinks on the floor. The place looks surprisingly neat inside. To my surprise, they have a bottle of homemade vodka. The label promises "White Label Scotch Whisky" but is full of spelling mistakes. There is also a bottle of fake, alcohol-free Heineken. I show them pictures of the original product but they've never heard of Heineken. The alcohol hits me right away because I haven't had a drink in months. After a few rounds I fall into a deep sleep.

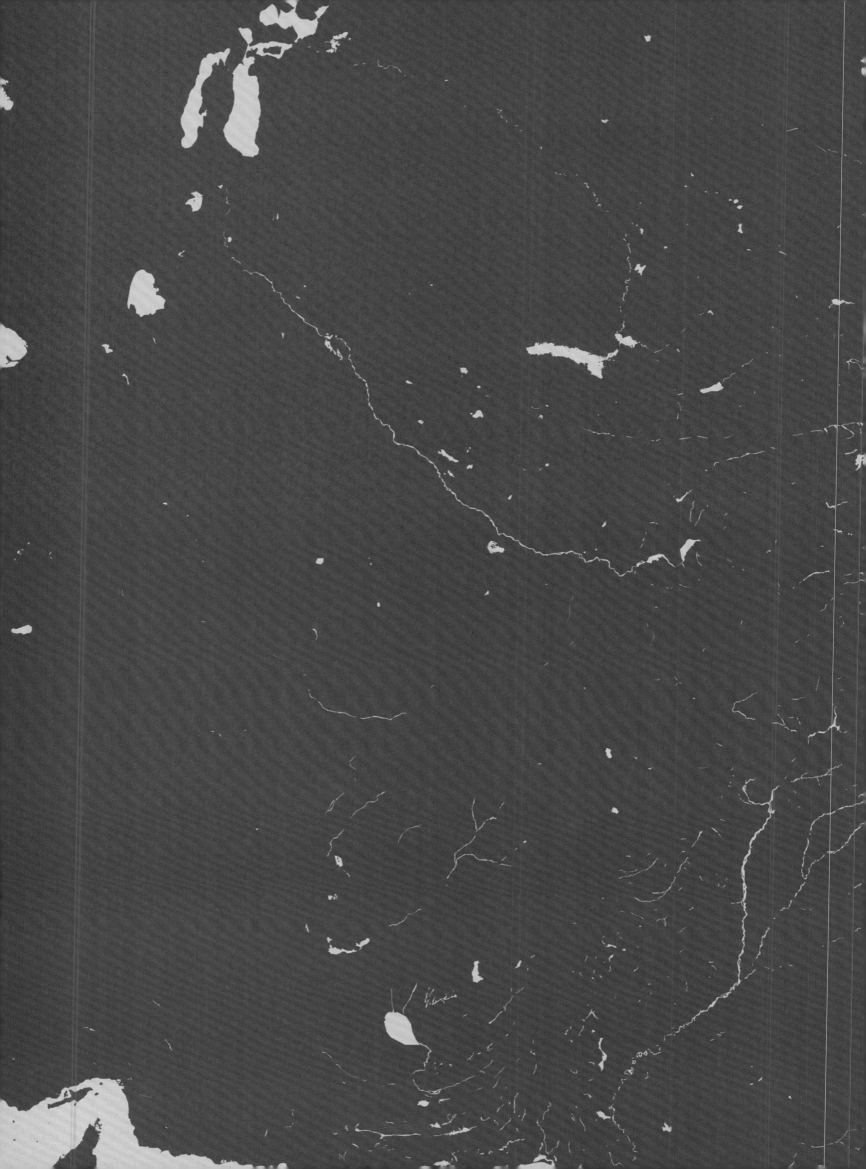

CENTRAL ASIA

DAY 146 - 8260 KM

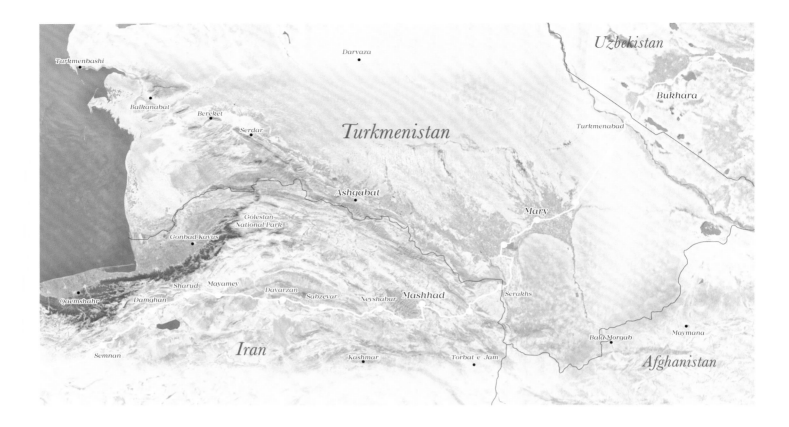

500 km in 5 days

Turkmenistan is tougher, hotter, drier, and more desolate than Iran. I thought I'd already done my share of desert riding in Iran, but I was wrong. My transit visa allows me just five days to cross the country to Uzbekistan, covering 500 km, mainly through desert.

According to the hotel manager in Sarakhs, the last town in Iran, the border opens at 7 a.m. I get up early, but around 8 a.m. there is still nobody on the Iranian side. There are lots of people but not the person who is responsible for immigration. The passports, mostly green ones from Turkmenistan, are piled up, waiting to be stamped, with my burgundy Dutch one on top. Finally after an hour of waiting someone passes the line. "Mister Martin, you can come." He checks a few of my bags and wants to see my photos. All good—I can go. On the Turkmenistan side, things are more complicated. I have to take my bike into a large white marble building. On the wall there's a futuristic-looking painting of the capital Ashgabat with majestic white and gold buildings. Everyone is in green, the national color of Turkmenistan. Many times I need to show my passport. I get stamps here and there, pay immigrant fees, and everything is written by hand into a big book. After a total of three hours I cross the border. Country number 11.

I cycle to the only nearby town to get some groceries, but the ATM doesn't work. Later I find out I can't use my credit cards in Turkmenistan. Luckily I have some U.S. dollars left, but it's a poor situation. I should prepare better next time; now I need to live on small rations each day until I find a bank. Maybe in Uzbekistan.

The school is out and a swarm of young kids surrounds me. Boys in neat black trousers, white shirts, and black ties, and girls in long, green dresses with colorful backpacks. All the women I see are beautifully dressed in elegant, colorful dresses reaching to the ground. Naturally beautiful and without any make-up. Such a contrast with the Iranian fashions. I'm a bit startled by the money situation and the new sights so I forget to take pictures. Alright, on with the trip. I shouldn't get distracted. I need to make 100 km today and it's already noon.

Out of town the road starts to get really bad and it stays like that. Deep cracks and potholes. The sun burns relentlessly. Flat land under a bowl of blue. Nothing but sand and bushes left and right. I haven't seen clouds for days. The water in my water bag is still ice cold and tastes so good that I want to drink liters all at once. The road is so bad that there are barely any cars. Once an hour a truck passes by at reduced speed, trying to avoid the potholes in the road.

After 50 km there's a road block where I have to show my passport. The gold-toothed cops are friendly, and I take a moment to rest in the shade; there is no chance to hide from the sun anywhere else. These are going to be five long days.

↑ Radio interview on the road leaving Iran.

The worst day of the trip

Mary, one of the larger towns in Turkmenistan, is where I spend my second night in a hotel. I've cycled 115 km and I'm totally exhausted. Although I'm on schedule, the five-day deadline is pressing on me. The bed is so comfortable that I can't get myself motivated to get up the next morning. I leave Mary in the burning heat. From here it will only be sand for 200 km and the opportunities to get water are scarce. On Google Maps I see the last village approaching. Off the main road I ask people for su (water) and they point me further into the village. I end up in a yard, but there is no store. One man is happy to fill up my water bag and his family surrounds me. I also ask for some eggs for my protein breakfast, and a woman offers me bread and eggs. When I pull out my wallet they refuse any payment. I give them my business card and take a family portrait. A picture they will never have because there is no internet in this town. Still, it's a way to show gratitude. As I cycle on, it gets dark, and I pick a sand dune not far from the road to set up my tent and spend the night.

The fourth day I get up at 5 a.m. and my stomach is not feeling too well. Breakfast consists of two eggs, black tea, peaches, and dry bread, which I dip in sesame spread and tea to make edible. The sun gets hot right at sunrise, but the air is still fresh. Until 10 a.m. the temperatures will be fairly mild. After that it's like cycling through an oven. My tongue dries out from the constant headwind, no matter how much I drink. The water in my water bag is now warm and it leaves a weird taste in my mouth. Shiny, bright-green Tuborg bottles lay on the side of the road, smiling at my thirsty face—empty, of course. My stomach is still not doing well, and I need to make some emergency stops. Then I find a tent with three old ladies knitting camel puppets and selling ice-cold camel milk. I stop and drink a whole bottle at once. It's the most delicious thing in the world. After that it gets so hot that I feel weak and my speed drops to 10 km/h. I decide to hitchhike. A small truck stops. I ask, pointing at my stomach, if he can take me to Turkmenabad. In the back of his truck there are gas flasks, so for safety reasons he can't carry the bike. He gives me some aspirin and I decide to cycle on. Slowly, with more breaks. Every 15 minutes I reward myself with a water shower. With the wind blowing in my face, this is so refreshing that it's the thing I keep looking forward to. Each time, though, I'm totally dry again after two minutes. Now my hair is hard from the dust and

dried water. Just before sunset a café pops up on the horizon, and when I arrive I order a beer. I stretch and lie down on a topchan*. Best moment of the day. I cycle on till dark, and after I've dragged my bike through the soft sand I am almost too tired to set up the tent. Luckily there are no mosquitoes, so I lie on my back for an hour staring at the countless stars.

> Insects jump against the tent, looking for a warm place. I hear them creeping under the groundsheet.

In the night the wind dies and the silence is almost loud. It creeps me out sometimes. All the little noises you make are magnified in the silence. I think of a story I read of someone sleeping in the desert and having a camel spider jump on his sleeping bag. He had left the zippers open. I never leave the zippers open, no matter how hot it is, and double check they're closed. The idea of scorpions and huge spiders in my tent gives me the shivers. The only warm place in the desert right now is where I am. Tomorrow I have to be at the border.

I wake up feeling better but the saddle pain I had in Iran is coming back again. I don't know what is wrong, maybe the position of my saddle changed somehow. Or maybe the number of hours is more than I can handle. I normally can't sit on a chair for a couple of days. At the border, things go terribly slow. All my bags are being checked thoroughly. Photos need to be shown, laptops examined, wallets checked. I have to fill out a form to declare how much money I'm bringing into Uzbekistan. It's my last 20 dollars. When I leave the country I'm not allowed to take more than that— a very strange rule. Although there is air-conditioning, I sweat like crazy. Blood is still pumping through my body from the last sprint to be on time. Other travelers are staring at me; I must look like I'm on heroin or something. After crossing the border to Uzbekistan I stop a taxi to take me to Bukhara, where I will rest for a while. It can't get any worse than this. Physically, I have reached my limits.

*Wooden dinner table / bench that is widely seen in cafés and restaurants in Central Asia.

Bukhara has a history that goes back millennia. The city is one of the oldest along the Silk Road and historically was part of the Persian empire. The city's center—which is the site of many mosques and 17th-century madrasas—is a UNESCO World Heritage Site.

Bukhara
Resting up in Uzbekistan

For the first time on this trip I stay in a hostel. Every day that I wasn't camping I'd booked a hotel or stayed in people's homes. I've survived the long trek through Turkmenistan and now enjoy some time off, meeting a lot of fellow travelers. They are mostly backpackers and an occasional tramp on a bike. Most people are on the road for a longer period; if you're visiting these countries, it's usually not for a weekend trip. It's nice to be in the social environment of a hostel again. I remember staying in hostels in New York, San Francisco, Chicago, London, and Berlin. Cheap, dirty rooms, often occupied by loud and drunk tourists. The past years I used sites like Couchsurfing and Airbnb a lot. I guess I was tired of sleeping in smelly dormitories with snoring people around me. The hostels here appear to be very nice. They also attract different types of travelers than the city backpackers in Europe and the U.S. It's not just those who are out to party.

After the 500 km "race" through Turkmenistan I am totally fed up with cycling. An ongoing saddle pain was torturing me so I'm taking seven days of rest in Bukhara, a small historic city in west Uzbekistan. Bekh runs the Rumi Hostel here, together with his parents, and takes care of you like you're part of the family. Great breakfast, fresh fruit, coffee and tea served throughout the day. They've helped me to get a local SIM card and all kinds of other stuff. I can enjoy small luxuries like alcohol, good food, and uncensored internet. I can finally update my blog again. Things I normally take for granted but haven't had access to for two months. I visit the same restaurant every day. I try the whole menu and in the end they know what I like. Bukhara has a lot of touristy sights, but I don't feel like exploring the city that much. If you've been a tourist for five months, you don't feel the urge to explore all the time. I'm tired of being a tourist. Tired of cycling, tired of camping, tired of being on the road. I just want a place where I feel at home.

The weather gets colder, like a late summer's day in the Netherlands. The sun is less warm and the cold breeze that comes with the Jewish New Year in Uzbekistan has struck up. I stroll around the old city and kill time chatting with other travelers. Talking about getting visas for the next countries and staring at smartphones waiting for the slow internet to load my news feed. It's what people do in hostels and what I need right now.

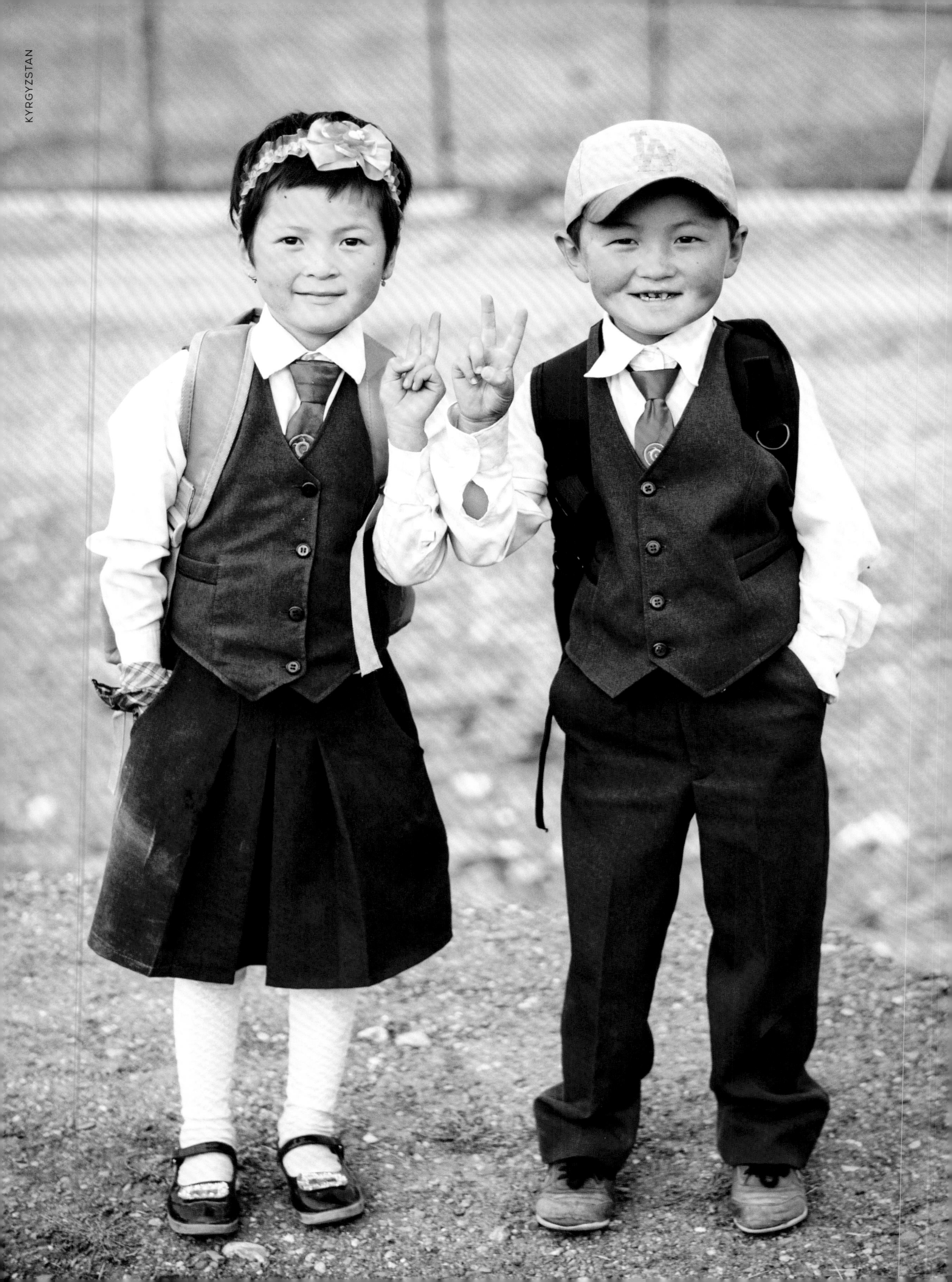

Rich & poor

> "The best way to find out
> if you can trust somebody
> is to trust them."

On the way through the backcountry of Kyrgyzstan, I passed villages where people live simple lives in small homes, mostly without running water. From a Western point of view, we would probably call them "poor," but I've never experienced it like that. These people don't have much but they seem happy. They have plenty of food and water, are surrounded by the beauty of nature, and have playful children scattering around the house. The little ones make a habit of frantically running after me and cheering "Hello" and "Goodbye" till I am out of sight. Most of the children I see walking to and from school are alone or in pairs and always without their parents. Apparently, being on their own poses not much of a risk. Few let their children walk to school alone in Western cities.

In this simpler way of life there is a certain carelessness. For example, there are barely any fences. Donkeys, sheep, cows, and horses roam the streets freely. This is such a contrast with where I am from. In the Netherlands everything is done according to script. Fences and markings divide private spaces from public areas. Rules are written for everything. If you would like to plant a tree in your yard or build an extra window in your attic, you have to ask permission from the municipality. Of course, those regulations have their purpose in some ways, but they must sound ridiculous to the people here. It's the same with traffic. There doesn't seem to be any real rules here, yet everything appears to work fine. Once you understand the rhythm, things go smoothly and you fit in.

And what about privacy and hospitality? I found that the poorest people seemed to share the most. They invited me to their homes for dinner or offered me a bed, without knowing me at all or expecting something in return.

As a child I learned to watch out for strangers, to distrust people you don't know, because they might do you harm. It seems that the more "civilized" people are, the more anxious they are towards strangers. With the majority of the people in Iran, Turkey, and Central Asia I've experienced the opposite. Don't get me wrong, I feel privileged to live in a country like the Netherlands, and it's almost impossible to compare the different cultures. I'm also not saying one or the other is better. Both societies have their own problems, but the experiences I've had with people on this trip have been eye opening. To quote Hemingway: "The best way to find out if you can trust somebody is to trust them." We can be so prejudiced and feel that we know what's happening in the world from what we read in the news, but really we have no idea. Beyond the perspective the Western news provides us, there is a much larger world, from which I am just experiencing the tiniest bit. One thing I have learned is that happiness doesn't have anything to do with being rich or poor.

What's next?

When I left Amsterdam in spring, I didn't have much more of a plan than to cycle east. I said I was going to China because the place sounded big and far away. At this point, after 10,000 km, I've reached Kyrgyzstan and the Chinese border is just a few days away. But this trip has never been about reaching China. It's about everything in between. With winter coming, I decide to take a plane to India and continue my journey eastwards from there. Of course it would be ideal if I could cycle the whole way, but it's simply not possible (or safe enough) to cross Afghanistan, Pakistan, and Tibet on a bike.

One other big highlight of this trip that I was looking forward to is the Pamir Highway in Tajikistan. It's one of the most scenic roads on earth, running high through the northern part of the Himalayas. I wanted to apply for a visa in Tehran, but it took too long, so I let it go. Yesterday I flew to Bishkek to give it another shot at the Tajik embassy, but they ran out of passport visa stickers, so no there was Tajik visa for me. With the Indian visa I had more luck. Today I will leave Osh (south Kyrgyzstan) on the bike and will cycle to the Tajik border on the Pamir Highway, which is at 4,200 m altitude. From there I will cycle back north to Bishkek, where I will take a plane to India. The latest weather reports showed extreme temperatures of -15°C during the nights so I'm expecting to return with pictures of snow.

Dark skies, high altitudes

I had heard the Pamir Highway was one of the most spectacular mountain roads through Central Asia but also the most physically demanding route because its altitude rises above 4,000 m. I was unfortunate when I applied for a Tajik visa. Because of some recent shootings, visas stopped being issued to tourists. I could only cycle the Kyrgyzstan part of the highway: 185 km uphill from 900 to 3,600 m to the Tajik border, and back again.

Kyrgyzstan is a paradise for wild camping. The landscape is so remote that it's easy to find a spot. The hot summer days were behind me, so I didn't have to get in the saddle before sunrise to skip the heat of the day. At night it got cold. I hadn't made a fire since Turkey, simply because there was no wood anywhere. I was happy to use my axe again—a piece of equipment that I'd carried but only used twice in Germany in early spring. I love the coziness and heat of a campfire. It makes any camp feel

more like home. If I hadn't eaten yet, I'd cook up some noodles or pasta. I'd walk around camp, take some photos, read a bit on my Kindle. At a gas station they sold some local cognac—perfect for the colder hours of my stay. The only sounds were the river, flowing swift and strong, and the crackling of the fire. It felt really peaceful.

This was when I found out my sleeping mat had a puncture and I had to spend some nights sleeping on the ground, which was not very pleasant. I suppose this had to happen sooner or later after all those nights in thorny deserts.

As I made progress on the M41,* the roads got steeper and the air thinner. The fourth day I reached the highest point on the Taldyk Pass at 3,615 m. The weather was grim but the moment joyful. Another personal record. It was hailing and snowing

*The M41 is also known as the Pamir Highway. It is 2,038 km long and crosses the Pamir Mountains, running through the countries of Afghanistan, Uzbekistan, Tajikistan, and Kyrgyzstan. It is the only continuous road through the mountains, but its terrain varies greatly. The route itself has been used for thousands of years and was part of the ancient trade route, the Silk Road.

when I cycled down to Sary Tash, my last village stay in Kyrgyzstan, where I would spend the night. When I stopped at the first guesthouse, my feet were frozen and I was shivering from the cold descent. They offered me a room without heating, but warmth was my first priority. The host was a girl in her twenties who lived with her grandparents. When I made clear how cold I was, she took me to a room facing the kitchen with a wall stove.

"Thank you. Where can I find the shower?"
"*Shower is 100 som (€1.20) extra. Only cold shower.*"
No way, I thought to myself.
"Can I warm up some water then with this boiler?"
There was a water boiler in the hallway.
"*I'll ask my grandmother.*"
She left the room.
"*You can use the shower tonight, but my brother has to fix it first.*"
Later in the evening I asked if the shower was ready.
"*My grandmother doesn't want you to use the shower.*"

"Really? You must be joking! Listen, I have cycled all day. My clothes are wet, and I am freezing cold. I really would like to use the shower."
She frowned for a second.
"*OK, come with me.*"

We walked outside in the dark. She carried two buckets of water and I followed her to a shed. Inside I found a do-it-yourself built-in shower with a reservoir on top. She climbed on a bench and emptied the buckets into the reservoir, pushed a button connected to some wires to the reservoir, and then said: "*In 30 minutes you can shower.*" Later I went back. It was cold in the shed, but the water was nice and warm. I think I've never enjoyed a warm shower as much as that one. I wondered why her grandmother wouldn't let me use the shower. Maybe the electricity was too expensive, which is hard to believe. I had no idea.

The next morning the sun was white and bright and warmed up my day. In the village everything was peaceful and quiet.

The stillness of high altitude overwhelms you. Cold, thin air, dry grass, the absence of life. From the porch I could look over the village and the huge plains lying ahead towards Tajikistan. I had a decision to make. Cycle to the border on the pass, 30 km ahead, or go back from here. My sleeping mat was punctured so sleeping on the ground in the freezing cold at 4,000 m was getting less attractive than it already was. I packed my bags and cycled down the empty road for about 10 km. The scenery didn't change one bit. There was no traffic. No wind. Nothing. Only the sun, the straight empty road, and the silence. I stepped off and sat in the middle of the road for a few minutes, looking at the vast mountain range, the so-called "roof of the world." I daydreamed for a while and a great feel-

ing of peace came over me. I was totally exposed in the open field but at the same time completely isolated in the infinity of the landscape. Maybe people could see me, but it would be from at least 10 km away.

I pedaled back to Sary Tash, did some grocery shopping, and prepared for the ride back to Osh. On the Taldyk Pass at midday it was warm and sunny. Two large vultures patrolled the sky above. When cycling down I met two hikers from Switzerland who were on their way to China on foot. They'd left in January and would reach the border in four days or so. Insane. We chatted for a while and they went on, upwards. For me it was going to be downhill for the next three days, back to Osh.

The Pamir Highway through Afghanistan, Uzbekistan, Tajikistan, and Kyrgyzstan. (For route cycled, see p. 221.)

I was totally exposed in the open field but at the same time completely isolated in the infinity of the landscape.

Mountains cover over 80% of Kyrgyzstan. The country is known for the many wild horses and donkeys living in the valleys.

Taldyk Pass

Soviet charm

I'm in the final part of Kyrgyzstan before I fly to India. From Osh to Bishkek I'm on a single 650-km road through a remote landscape. The first days I pass through the suburbs and little villages that connect the two bigger cities, but after that the road gets quiet. I hear my chain screaming for a drop of oil and give it what it needs. I've been cycling with this chain since Istanbul, so it's getting pretty worn out. I camp in the field right next to the Uzbek border. Memories come back as I wave at the cotton pickers on the other side of the fences getting into buses. We're all done working for the day. I pitch my tent, build a fire, and the rest of the evening I'm busy maintaining it. Light and warmth are basic necessities to work for. Life can be so simple.

The next day, mountains start rising up from the ground, and for two days I cycle along a reservoir lake with the greenest water I've ever seen. The road goes up and down the mountain slopes without gaining much altitude. Tough on the legs but very pleasing to the eyes. I enjoy the cold, fresh air and the earthy colours of autumn. The short transition from a hot summer to a long winter is exhilarating. After four days of camping I end up in a town (Karakul) and decide to check into a hotel. I could use a shower, and I have to do a bit of work on my laptop so I can take my mind off the road. The skies turn gray, and when I check the weather, they say it will be raining all night. Perfect timing for a hotel stay. The first one I find on my iPhone app doesn't seem to exist anymore; the second one is a run down Soviet complex. I walk in and an old lady helps me. The place is old and outdated. No wi-fi, no breakfast, but the room is cheap. The curtains, the furniture, the tablecloth—it all looks like grandmother's underwear. Outside it rains. It's all sadness. I ask if there is a kitchen so I can make myself some coffee. I follow the lady through a long corridor to a room which has an electric stove on a small table. That will do for me. I try to have zero expectations from hotels; I have seen the best and the worst on this trip.

There were stories of wild marijuana growing in the area.

I spend a lot of time staring at maps to see how the roads develop. When to expect inclinations, special sights, places to camp, towns in which to re-stock food. Lake Toktogul, a large reservoir in central Kyrgyzstan, was getting nearer and looked substantial on the map. There were stories of wild marijuana growing in the area. The M41—more or less the only road I've been cycling in Kyrgyzstan—goes around the lake. It was a stiff climb to get there. Some trucks along the road wait for their engines to cool. I feel for them: the old trucks, battling themselves up the steep hills with crying engines. Sometimes I'm faster. Most of them are old trucks from Germany, still with their original logos. I didn't find marijuana, but I saw several C&A trucks shipping hay with people on top, which was a pretty funny sight.

Kyrgyzstan became independent from the Soviet Union in 1991. In some parts you'll find completely abandoned villages. Between the 1930s and 50s, several industrial towns were built deep in the heart of Kyrgyzstan's Tian Shan Mountains. Once proud, busy industrial settlements, today they are places full of rowdy characters who are strangers in their own landscape. The towns are now filled with silence and nostalgia.

9693 KM KARAKOL

221

Extreme days

After Lake Toktogul the road rose up from 1,000 to 3,000 m. There were two high peaks to climb and then a long descent down to Bishkek, my final destination in Kyrgyzstan. The weather forecast wasn't promising, but I was looking forward to seeing some snow at the top. As soon as I began climbing, it started to rain. A continuous drizzle that didn't stop for two days.

There is no way to dress properly for this kind of weather. If you're wearing 100% waterproof rain gear, you'll get drenched with sweat, which will stay in your clothes. If you wear breathable, water-resistant clothing, you will get wet from the rain. My rain pants are 100% waterproof and have long legs that I can pull over my Palladiums. I like my shoes, but they are totally useless in extreme conditions. If there is water on the road, they get soaking wet in an instant because I don't have a mudguard on the front wheel anymore. It broke somewhere in Germany on the fourth day of the trip. On my upper body I wear a thin synthetic layer that enables sweat to evaporate quickly and my Fjällräven rain jacket. Two thin layers are warm enough because my inner furnace is at full capacity when I'm climbing. The jacket's G-1000 fabric is known for its ability to be water-resistant, breathable, and ultra fast drying at the same time. Of course, this is always a compromise. If water can get out, it can also get in. Wax is available to rub into the jacket to improve its water resistance. Still, during a full day of rain it's not going to protect you. The good thing was that above 2,500 m the rain slowly transitioned into snow and my clothes started to dry from my body heat. At the summit I was almost dry but had to keep moving to stay warm.

There was an abandoned shack where I could hide from the wind and snow to change my clothing. During a descent it's a lot colder due to the higher speed and the reduced physical effort. I was happy I bought a snow jacket a couple of weeks ago. I exchanged all my clothes for dry ones. Outside everything was white, even the sky. It snowed so hard I couldn't see beyond 100 meters. I had to put on sunglasses to keep the snow from going into my eyes. It was just below zero degrees, which made the snow sticky and watery. The dérailleur* of my bike got obstructed. Everything got covered in ice while I descended at 40 km/h. I had to stop several times to clean the dérailleur, change gears manually, and get the snow out of my face because I couldn't see a thing. My shoes had gotten all wet and my toes were freezing. After 20 km there were

*The unit that transports the chain from one cog to the next.

a few houses and a restaurant, which I reached using the last gear that still worked, as most parts of my bike were frozen solid with ice and snow.

Inside it was nice and warm, and I started to take off all my wet clothes while being stared at by the staff of the small restaurant. Outside it got dark, with the snow still falling in vast amounts. I asked if I could put the bike inside to thaw out, but the restaurant owner was not happy with that idea. Understandably, because the ice and dirt would have made quite a mess. There was a space under the restaurant where the sheep stayed that was also warm. I followed a boy around the house through the snow. I couldn't stand up straight and there was mud everywhere. In the middle was a big stove that heated the entire restaurant. I parked the bike next to it so it could spend a warm night. To my surprise, I found out the restaurant was a hotel, and they offered me a bed. But that was all there was. No shower, and the toilet was outside in the snow. I asked the boy if he could warm up some water so I could wash myself. The rest of the evening I spent in front of a small TV watching Kyrgyz music videos.

Staying in a hotel helped. Both the bike and my toes warmed up well. After breakfast I continued through the white landscape. It didn't snow anymore. I calculated it would take two days to get to Bishkek. One more climb to go. Around 5 p.m. I started the climb, which meant I would be camping at high altitude. In two hours I had climbed 700 m, something I couldn't imagine I was able to pull off when I started my trip. At the top I went through a narrow tunnel for 3 km. Luckily there was not much traffic. The noise and the polluted air in a tunnel are far from pleasant. After the tunnel I found the perfect place to camp: right on the edge of the mountain with a view of the road creep

ing down between the cracks of the mountain. I had a slight problem being without a light source. I'd lost my head-light somewhere and my phone had died. I tried to charge it with my laptop, but I couldn't wake it up in the cold. It was surprising to see how all my electronic devices failed in freezing conditions. I was lucky there was a half-moon that lit my camp, but it was only for a couple of hours before it disappeared behind the mountains. I had to cook up some food in complete darkness. Building a fire was not an option because there was no wood. I was walking around all the time to keep my feet warm. The wind got stronger which made it really cold. One of my bags got

All my electronic devices failed
in freezing conditions.

blown off the cliff so I had to climb down a bit to retrieve it. My
speedometer showed 7°C in the evening with temperatures
rapidly dropping. Still, I was excited because of the spectacular view and the extreme circumstances. It felt powerful and
adventurous. When I went to bed, I put on all my clothes and
pulled my snow jacket over my head. It was far from comfortable but more or less warm. My breath froze on the inside of
the tent while the wind was trying to blow my tent off the cliff.
I didn't sleep much. It was a long night. Early in the morning
I got up, skipped breakfast, packed up, and started on the
125-km-long descent towards Bishkek.

During my last days in Central Asia I cycled in the most extreme weather conditions. Like the first days, when I was exposed to the hot desert climate of Turkmenistan. One reason I started this trip was to push myself through limits. I left Kyrgyzstan with a great feeling of accomplishment.

INDIA

DAY 194 - 10032 KM

Home in Arambol, Goa.

A new beginning

India. Could there be a bigger contrast to Kyrgyzstan? The climate, the culture, the religion, the people. I jumped into a totally different world. I landed in India with basically no plan, other than that I was tired of traveling and needed time off to write, work, and, more importantly, stay put for a while. I wanted to be in one place again to reset my mind. I stayed in Delhi for three days to work on my photo and video material. There was so much I'd captured along the way. So many small moments and experiences I had already forgotten about. Life is rich and intense when you travel.

After talking with my friend Riri on the phone, I made up my mind how to approach India. She was in India too. We would meet each other in Goa. From there, I would continue my journey eastbound through India. My bike was still in the cardboard box they had used in transit. Delhi was pleasantly warm; Goa was hot and humid when I arrived at midnight. Covered in sweat, I put the bike back together at the airport in Vasco da Gama. I had clearly gotten used to the cold, dry air of autumn in Central Asia. India was like a different planet. I cycled to Arambol, a small village on the coast of north Goa where I would later meet Riri. I stayed in a small apartment at the edge of the village, close to the beach. A quiet neighborhood surrounded by palm trees, banana plants, and the occasional monkey eating the fresh leaves in my yard. I started working on the photo book of my trip. In the morning I had breakfast on the porch, worked a bit, went to the beach for a swim, and then got back to work.

There were a lot of restaurants, but I ate only at Laughing Buddha and returned there every day because everything tasted so good. I developed daily rituals, making life simple and trying to live like I would at home. I really needed that simple rhythm for a few days. There was just zero interest in new things. At the end of one day, I took the bike to the beach and cycled on the hard sand a couple of miles south. It cleared my mind, gave me perspective. The sound of the waves, the wide open space, no traffic, the sun dying in the haze on the horizon, the warm wind making the palm trees whisper. I took everything slowly and felt at ease.

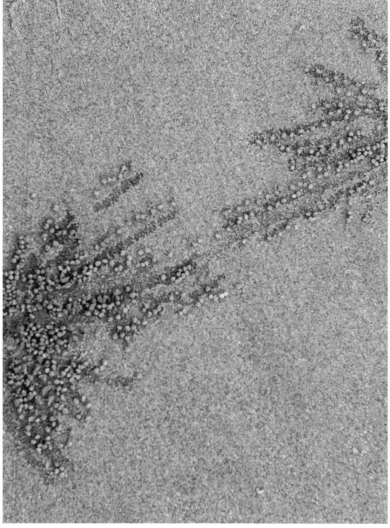

I was happy with the progress I had made on my book and was looking forward to seeing Riri again. I'd met her in New York the year before. We have completely different backgrounds. Me being brought up in a safe and isolated Christian environment in a small town in the south of Holland. She, raised in Paris, being the daughter of an American photo model and an Indian father. Having studied, and worked in New York and Milan as a model, she had now taken another path: as a fashion designer and yoga teacher in India. Quite a big change, which made our time together even more interesting. We had so many stories to tell. A great start to a well-deserved vacation.

Days were totally random. We lingered in the water like there was no tomorrow.

The beach was only a three-minute walk away from our little house. A small path went through overgrown backyards full of palm trees and tropical plants. Because the tourist season had not started yet, we had a lot of beaches just to ourselves. The high waves brought out the inner children in us. Days were totally random; we lingered in the water like there was no tomorrow and roamed freely on the beach like the painted cows. Life can be so carefree.

Arambol is a typical Goan place. It's somewhat westernized and it can be touristy, but there is a laidback vibe. Yoga places, organic cafés, tantric meditation classes—you'll find it all there. The 60s hippie generation that settled there is still present. We visited this place called Once in Nature, an organic restaurant with live music. People were sitting on the floor in a dimly lit, open space among the palm trees. There was a small stage where musicians played all kinds of instruments. Men with wooden jewelry and skirts, who answered to names like "White Dove." Peculiar folks with open minds and connected souls. No alcohol or meat was served, but weed was all over the place. We'd hang out there almost every evening. There were open music nights so I took along a guitar that I had bought on the beach to play a few notes with the band. I also performed a few Lou Reed songs myself. It'd been a while since I had been on stage. I was a little rusty on the guitar, but it was fun.

Goa is a tranquil place. The damp hot air brings a certain lightness which makes you float. Everything happens slower. On Sunday morning we took a long ride on our scooter, hopping from village to village over the tropical green hills around Arambol and jumped into the water where the road touched the sea. You could say, what happens in Goa, stays in Goa. Time will tell what I'll take with me and what I'll leave behind.

The nightly jungle

The rain forest was loud at night. Big insects fluttered against my head, monkeys howled from the trees, eyes in the forest lit up in my head-light.

I'd left Goa around noon, hot-headed after spending an hour in a camera store arguing with the salesman while trying to return a newly bought Panasonic GH4. The one I'd used and abused so far on this trip had stopped working after a splashy adventure in the sea. What was I thinking?! Surprisingly enough, after hours of sitting next to the hair dryer, it had woken up from its six-day coma. The new camera, which I had paid for in advance, had just arrived in the store and there was no way I could return the purchase. So now I am carrying two cameras. There is still a chance the old one will give in because of the amount of salt inside it.

In the morning I'd said goodbye to Riri. She was flying back to Mysore where she currently lives, and I would start my journey through India. The biggest country on this trip. Saying goodbye is never fun, but it was a joyous morning with an early swim and a good homemade breakfast on the porch. Our little house in Goa had grown on me. It's always hard to leave the safe harbor and get back on the lonely roads. And how lonely it is after some quality time with precious people. But I was excited and full of energy. I needed to bite the bullet and get on with my trip. Setting small goals and not getting frightened by the size of this country. Living by the day and taking it in piece by piece. It was the only way to make this kind of trip doable. My next goal was the far sea in the east. Seas had been my favorite goals on this journey. The Black Sea, the Sea of Marmara, the Caspian Sea, the Arabic Sea, and now the Bengal Sea. When I pedaled out of Arambol, the bike sounded like a wreck. Sand was still trapped in the chain and the salt water had left its rusty marks. The sea had been really good for me, but it had taken its toll on all of my gear. After some distance and a bit of oil between the joints the chain was back to normal.

At 10 p.m. I was still crawling up a hill. The palm trees were pitch black against the gloomy, dark blue sky. In the valley I could still see the fuzzy lights of villages I had passed. Further back, buried in the nocturnal haze of the rain forest, was the sea. I couldn't really see much, but I sensed a great view. I looked over my shoulder and said goodbye to the sea. It was hot and everything was sticky. I was hoping to find a camp spot soon, but the forest was too dense and there wasn't a flat space to pitch a tent. After passing a road sign welcoming me to a tiger reserve, I felt less comfortable with the idea of camping. But I had no choice, there were no hotels in the nearby area. No service on my phone either. After 700 m of climbing I reached a plateau. I took a small dirt road into the forest and found a place to call home. It had gotten pretty late and I was exhausted so I poured a bottle of water over myself as some sort of shower and zipped myself into the tiny tent. In the morning I woke up and was relieved to find myself not having been eaten by tigers.

There are signs that show you're on the right path.

Checking in at a hotel in Srikakulam.

India at my feet

I t's Diwali, the festival of light, in India. Trucks and cars are colorfully decorated, cattle of all types are painted, and there are fireworks in the most unpredictable places. People are happy and it's a great week to get to know India.

I spend a lot of time on the road. The traffic is like an arena fight, worse than I have ever experienced before. Turkey was a big change compared to Europe. In Istanbul I got hit by a car from the side but stayed in the saddle. It was the only time I got close to an accident on this trip. Iran, and in particular Tehran, brought a new dimension of traffic chaos I had to get familiar with. Where European traffic is based on following the rules, Asian traffic is based on rhythm and harmony. If you don't get into the groove, you'll get into accidents.

Traffic-wise, India tops all the places I've been to so far. One reason is because there are just so many more people. Whenever you think you're in a remote area, there is always someone around, chopping some coconuts, or just taking a crap in the middle of the road (yes, that really happened). Then there is the habit of using the horn while you approach. All vehicles play

the loudness game. It's like a swarm of seagulls around a fishing ship, with me being the ship. The worst are the trucks which flank you with deafening melodies that make your ears hurt.

> Asian traffic is based on rhythm and harmony. If you don't get into the groove, you'll get into accidents.

In India, traffic drives on the left, or let's say, is *supposed* to drive on the left. There are no rules for passing another vehicle—left or right, wherever there is a gap, they go. In slow traffic I was used to maneuvering in between the cars, which is a convenience of traveling by bike. In India that's not the case. Roads get totally clogged up when there is too much traffic and there is no way to get through. Motorcycles are all over the place, making up roughly 60% of the traffic. Occupied by

one, two, or sometimes a whole family, dog included. Many slow down a bit when they pass me and stare for a while. Most of them it's just for a minute, after which they carry on. Others linger a bit longer, watching from the back, the side, and the front, observing me as men can shamelessly look at a good-looking girl from head to toe. Others ask the regular questions, "Where you from?", "What's your name?", "Where you go?" Once their questions are answered, they move on without saying goodbye. There seems to be a different social etiquette. During stops it's not much different. Most of the time I'm cycling over roads where tourists never come. In restaurants along the road, at grocery stalls, hotel check-ins, everywhere people gather around the bike to have a look at something they have never seen before. A futuristic bicycle with all kind of accessories, fully loaded with bags in bright colors. Everything gets observed and touched like it's a time machine. And on the time machine sits an alien, with weird

long hair and a blond moustache. I imagine most people have only seen Western people on television, if they own one. So, how do I feel at the end of the day? Pretty tired. India is the most exhausting country to cycle through so far. The fact that I have no privacy takes up a lot of energy and I'm not even talking about the physical effort of pedaling through plus 30°C on bad roads.

It's not that I am not enjoying my time here, though. It's a magnificent country, full of surprises and unexpected things. As much as some people can challenge your temper, I have met some really lovely individuals as well. India can make or break your day and you won't see it coming. The food is amazing—everywhere—no doubt about that. Full of flavor and full of color. And everything else is like that. The nature, the culture, the spirituality. And for me, Diwali is a symbol for that. It's love over hate. There is no gray area, only vivid colors.

When I stopped in this little town, a crowd gathered around my bike, which
happened all the time in rural India. This little boy was shy and watching curi-
ously from a distance—hands in pockets, tie on the side—observing every move
I made without saying a word. I'd like to think he thought his outfit through in
detail before he stepped out of the door that morning. Bright little boy.

Aren't you scared?

One of the topics I'm often questioned about is spending the night alone in the wilderness. I've been camping in the strangest places: forests, beaches, gas stations, abandoned buildings, salt lakes, cornfields... People ask me all the time: Don't you feel scared, or alone?

The great thing about camping in the wild is that it opens your mind and sharpens the senses. I never feel more free to think about things than when I'm completely alone in nature, far from human influences. There are no distractions and boundaries, because there are no walls around you. At the same time you're alert to every sound, because you are exposed and unsheltered. It's natural behavior, but after some time you get used to things and you're able to better judge the safety of your surroundings. Still, anything can happen. I always take the time to get to know the area where I am camping. This time it's a beach, not far from the main road. First I park the bike and turn off all lights and wait. It's dark but there's a half moon. With my

head-light I go for a walk and explore the surroundings. Before setting up camp I sit down to take in the area. I listen to the silence. There are crickets and insects of all kinds: the usual sounds. The occasional noises from the road, further away. A motorcycle, a truck, a car. In the distance I hear an old diesel engine. Further away I hear some music and there seem to be voices somewhere. They come closer. I turn off my head-light and wait. There appears to be a house a few hundred meters away, and the wind plays with the direction of the sound. In the countryside it's so quiet that you are alerted to every little sound you hear. In the city there are so many noises that everything just becomes a blur and you hear nothing.

I feel comfortable. It's a good spot. Nothing fancy, just a place to sleep. It's a little after 9 p.m. I unpack my bags and start to set up camp. Everything is in its designated place, except I won't sleep in the tent this time. It's warm and there are no mosquitoes. From the first day I camped out in the woods of Hilversum, I stuck to the same routine. This way, I have everything within reach when I sit in front of my tent and the most valuable things, like my laptop bag, next to where I sleep. I heat up some water and pour it back in the bottle. This is my shower. Half a liter is enough to get fairly clean.

On a journey like this, your body is your only home, and you're exposed to everything.

Then I have another two hours to kill before bedtime. I walk around taking photos of little things. Weirdly enough I always find things to occupy myself, though at first I couldn't imagine what I would do without internet access or anyone to talk to.

At this point in my trip, I'm not scared anymore. In the beginning I felt a little nervous sleeping in dark forests and tropical jungles. I've had some scary moments with wild dogs, which are a threat in some countries. But I've learned how to deal with certain situations now. I've trained my ears and instinct to locate potential dangers. I don't feel loneliness. On the contrary: spending time in nature alone makes me feel stronger and more in harmony with myself. Fear can only be conquered if you face it and do not hide from it. Not overcoming obstacles only makes them bigger.

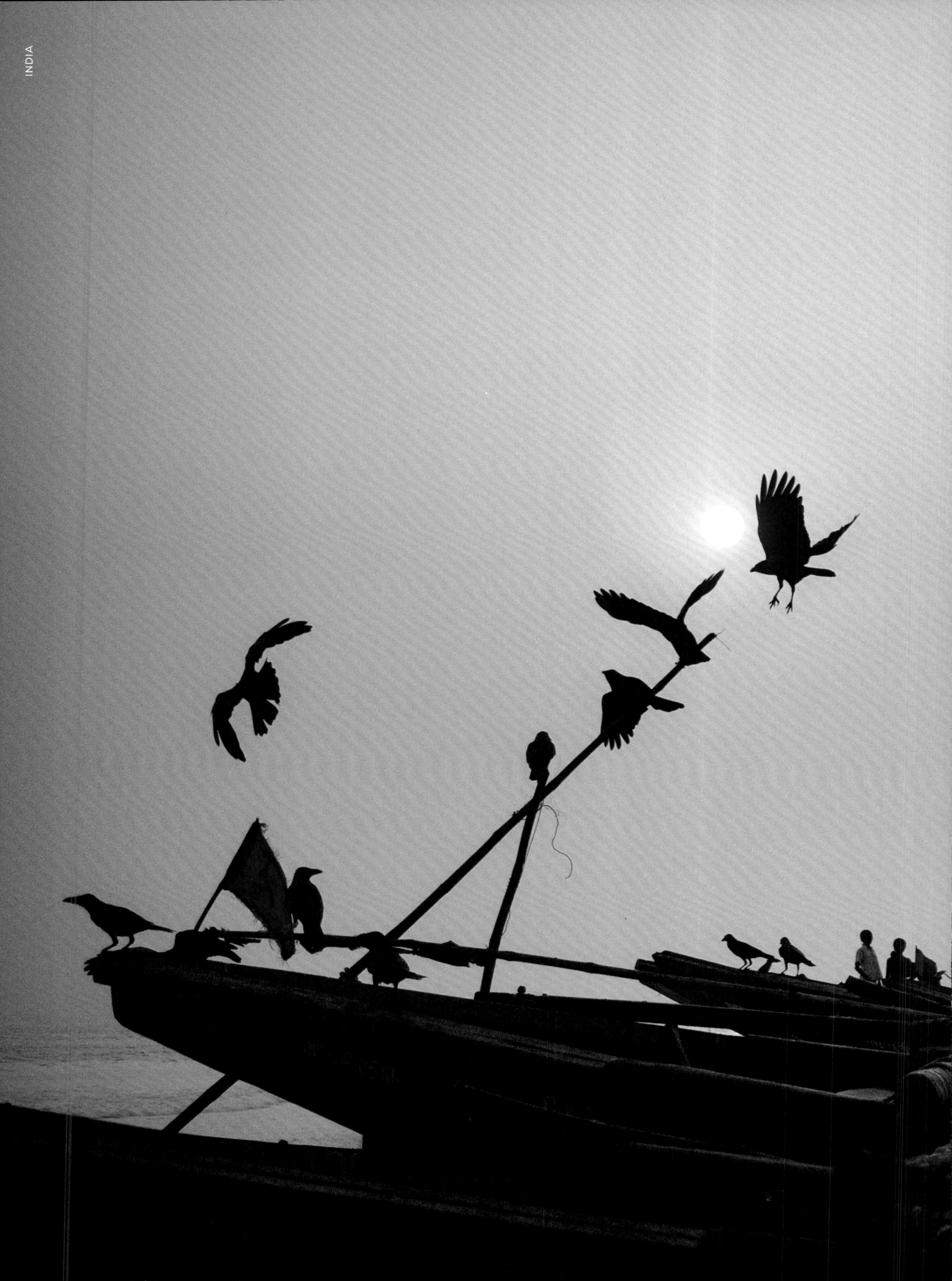

India has one of the largest railway systems in the world, with 115,000 km of tracks. It also has the longest platform: 1.4 km in Gorakhpur, Uttar Pradesh. Punctuality is often a challenge for Indian trains. The Guwahati-Trivandrum Express has held the record for the most delays in India, with an average of 10 to 12 hours.

Train ride
From Puri to Kolkata

In order to be at the border of Myanmar on time, I have to take a few trains to cover the distance in the two months my visa allows me to stay. To get a ticket for a bed, you need to make a reservation. On the day of a train's departure all reservations are closed, so I always end up buying a cheap ticket which gets me only into the general coaches that are cramped and dirty.

I take my bike directly onto the train, avoiding the hassle and paperwork of checking it in as a parcel. One time before, when I checked my bike in, I almost lost it, as it didn't get loaded onto the train. This time I have no idea if I'm allowed to take it onboard, but it is much more convenient this way. All the seats are full, and people are randomly sleeping on the floor and even on the baggage racks above the seats. I inflate my mattress and try to get some sleep on the cold metal floor. I have a hard time coming to rest. Partly because right next to me the toilets smell terrible. This is the worst train ride ever. At some point, during a stop at a bigger station, a lot of people get off, so I stumble with my six bags and guitar to one of the sleeper carriages, where I find an empty bunk bed and get some sleep.

At 5 a.m. the train rolls in at Kolkata Howrah Junction. It's misty and half dark from the polluted air. Around the station, people covered in blankets are sitting in the dirt around fires, warming themselves up with cups of tea while dogs sniff the surroundings. I feel I've arrived in the Wild West. I throw my bags on the platform and shudder at the scene, but at the same time I enjoy the adventure I'm again thrown into. It feels like I've gone back in time. Rubbish everywhere, old skinny men pulling wooden carts loaded with big parcels, rats creeping through the tracks, people washing themselves with the hoses designated for filling up the train reservoirs, and dust everywhere. I have to drag my bike over several tracks while steam trains slowly roll in. It's a scene I've only ever come across in movies.

Waking up in Kolkata

DAY 230 - 11460 KM

This morning around 7 a.m. I cycled into Kolkata. I thought I was in a dream, seeing this grim city come to life in a colorless haze of pollution. I hung my camera around my neck and took photos while I weaved my way through the madness.

Communal shower on the streets of Kolkata.

Kolkata, previously known as Calcutta, was once the capital of India.

The Hindustan Ambassador—the make of the yellow cab above—dominates the streets of
Kolkata. It was the first car produced in India and was in production from 1958 to 2014.

Like a black and white photo book of 60s New York that transports you to a different world, Kolkata seemed to be from another space and time.

↑ In Kolkata, hand-pulled rickshaws are still used.

Right after I leave my apartment I'm thrown back into the reality of life on the road. The traffic is worse than ever. The roads are too narrow for the amount of cars and motorbikes. Or it might be that India is too small for the number of people. It takes me half a day to get out of the city, but even then, it's still crowded. The roads get worse. Deep potholes and only scarce strokes of tarmac. Similar to Turkmenistan but now also filled with traffic. Everyone is fighting for some space. Several times I get pushed off the road by trucks. The skies are smoggy and dense, and my eyes dry out from the dust. It's a battlefield where motorcycles, rickshaws, cars, trucks, cows, goats, and crippled dogs rush past each other, like in a post-apocalyptic movie scene. In the bottom right photo I'm having a quick stop for some tea. I am slowly starting to get annoyed by the people in India. Basically, everywhere I make a stop, I have zero privacy. This is an everyday situation, and there is nowhere to hide. In Iran there were similar situations, but Iranians are more respectful, smile more, and

Sometimes I'm close to losing my temper because there is no breathing space.

keep some distance. Here, people want to touch everything—my gear, my bike, my computer, my phone. I want to stay friendly but it's gradually getting harder. Sometimes I'm close to losing my temper because there is no breathing space.

The way I travel through India is quite different from the way most people do. The size of the country is substantial and there are a lot of special places to visit. India has a lot to offer. Most people take public transport to visit all these highlights. I am just visiting a handful of those places and most of the time I'm in between everything. In other countries I've really enjoyed being "nowhere" most of the time. It's good as you see an authentic side of a country that is away from the usual tourist locations and beaten paths. You experience the unexpected. Right now I have the feeling that this way of traveling slowly is negatively affecting my image of India, where there are so many beautiful things to see. I've built up an aversion to the people without having control over it. I'm closed off, which I regret because I haven't got any patience left to open up to potentially interesting experiences. But I guess that's just how it has to be right now.

On the other hand, I'm happy that I am traveling the way I do. I'm really going below the surface. It might not always be enjoyable, but I feel that what I experience is something very raw and intense. I've seen a side of India which most tourists never see. It is a wild place, playing tricks on me all the time. I will probably understand things better at a later date, but at this point I need to get out of this chaos as soon as possible.

Fed up

I spent four nights in Kolkata to apply for the Myanmar visa and do some design work. Something I really missed. Creating things, being productive. I rented an Airbnb apartment with everything I needed to focus. Best of all, it was silent. For the first time in months I did some shopping and found out that trousers fit a lot better than before my trip. There was a big mall close by where I enjoyed Western coffee with cheesecake and saw *Spectre* in the cinema. Time well spent in a comfy bubble, floating above the madness of Kolkata. A stark contrast with the past weeks on the road. I spent as much money in three days as I had in the past three weeks. Not that I lived excessively, but on rural Indian roads there is just not much to spend money on. As soon as you switch to Western-style city life, though, you pay a lot more for anything.

When I started climbing the mountains, everything changed. Both Sikkim—a small, north Indian state that's inhabited mostly by people of Nepalese origin—and the city of Darjeeling were a different world for me. There were smiling faces again, less traffic, and cleaner air. Among the green tea plantations in Darjeeling I regained the joy of traveling.

Darjeeling is a city located at a height of over 2,100 m above sea level in the Lesser Himalayas. It is well known for its tea industry and the Darjeeling Himalayan Railway, which is a UNESCO World Heritage Site.

11696 KM DARJEELING

In contrast to most of India, the states Manipur and Nagaland are largely Christian. There is a very high church attendance rate in both urban and rural areas.

Not driving home for Christmas

After recovering from a cold in Guwahati, I'm cycling through the last two states of India on my trip, Nagaland and Manipur. It feels like I've left India already. The infrastructure is "cow free," Chinese food is on the menus, the people are of Mongolian descent, and the main religion is Christianity.

It's cold outside, and a lot of people have a red star burning above their little houses. They are celebrating the birth of their Saviour. It's the first major Christian community I come across since I left Europe. It's fascinating to see how religion inspires the culture in such different ways everywhere around the world. You forget how much impact it has on all aspects of life. When I cycle through villages, people are singing Christmas songs. Familiar melodies with unknown words. It's an unusual mix of cultures. The spirituality of India soon seems far behind. Even into Myanmar, the main religion is Christianity. One thing I've realized is that culturally, ethnically, and geographically, borders don't really exist: countries fade into each other.

At the border to Myanmar there is a strong military presence on the road. Trucks full of soldiers who greet me with waves and cheers. Despite the hostile image of men with heavy artillery on top of their vans, everyone is in a good mood. I ask a soldier to take a picture of me at a panoramic corner on the road.

Looking back, India has been quite a trip. Late October I arrived in tropical Goa, which felt like paradise coming from the winter-stricken highlands of Kyrgyzstan. I took a two-week break to enjoy the tranquil beach life, which was pure bliss. It broke up the trip in a good and a bad way. I needed the rest, but it was difficult to get back in the saddle because my drive and focus seemed gone. It wasn't that I didn't want to see India, but I was reluctant to face those endless days of cycling again. China, the initial goal, had more or less been reached (I was 200 km from its border in Kyrgyzstan). I'd climbed the steepest mountains, cycled through the hottest deserts, and camped out in the freezing cold—the job felt done. It also felt like India was not really part of this trip because I arrived by plane. This definitely messed up my mindset. I cycled every inch of the first part of this trip, through Europe and the Middle East. The shift to an alternative mode of transport was much more of a deal breaker than I expected, because it spoilt the simplicity and beauty of this journey. I approached India differently and was forced to take trains to make the distance in the two months I had on my visa. In hindsight though, I do not regret that I didn't cycle the whole of this route. It was the most intense country to go through but, therefore, maybe also one of the most memorable ones. Despite the challenges, somehow I fell in love with the untamed culture, the people, the food, and the vibrant colors.

MYANMAR

DAY 251 - 12097 KM

Thanboddhay Phaya, Myanmar

Laykyun Sekkya Buddha

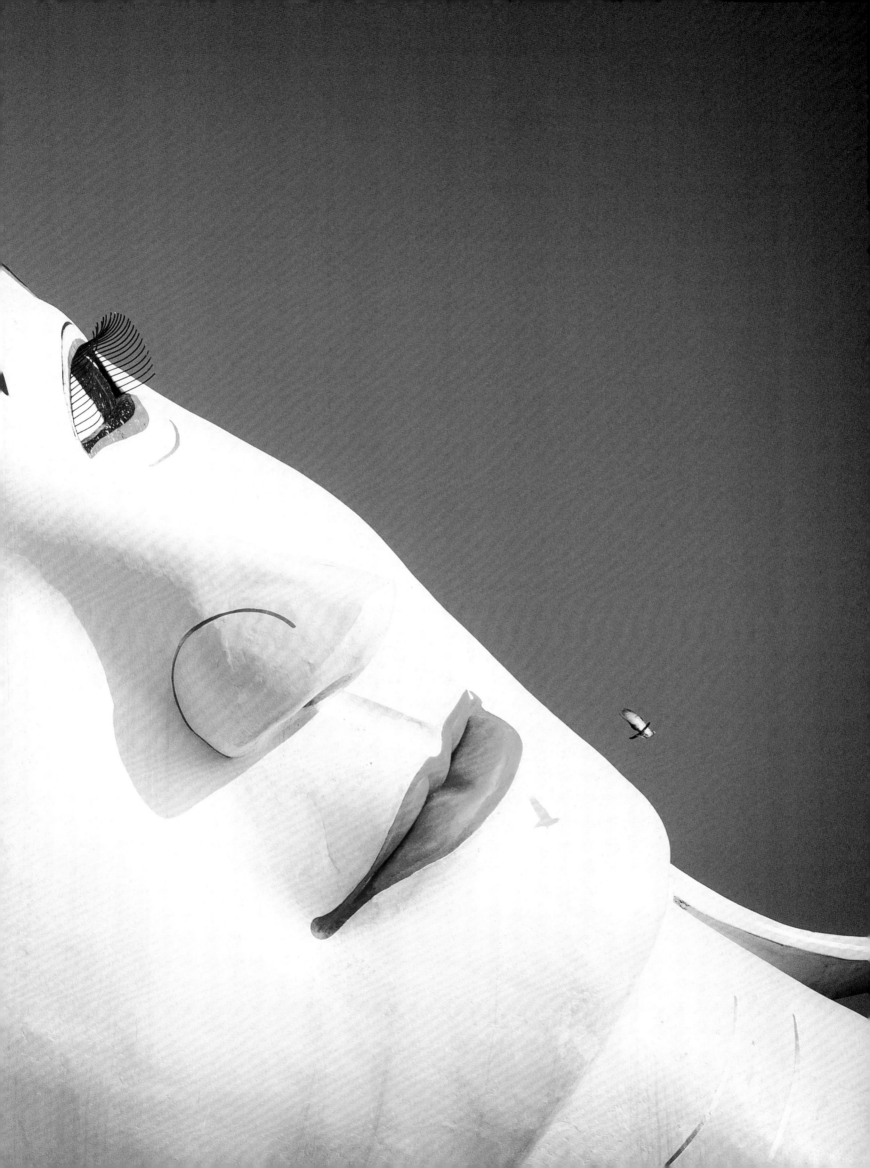

Burma

For years, Myanmar, also known as Burma, was closed to foreigners. Nowadays, tourism is rapidly increasing but mainly through organized tours to designated sites. The border crossing from India to Myanmar opened to foreigners just over a year ago. Still some provinces can't be visited independently and additional permits are needed. The northwest part of Myanmar is sparsely inhabited and the least developed. Most local people haven't seen foreigners before.

In the border town Tamu I buy a new SIM card and stock up on supplies. The first 150 km I am on the India-Myanmar Friendship Road, which is well paved. I cycle on till dark. I pass small villages with wooden houses in between giant trees. People walk slowly on the main road, coming back from their daily work on the fields. In my head light I only see the bottom part of their bodies. I see no faces. It's a spooky sight. When I take a break, all sounds are muted. A silence I didn't hear once in India. Every country has its own sounds. I recall the moments when I stood still in the dark with the bike between my legs, taking some sips of water. In Turkey I always heard prayers coming from the mosques. In Central Asia it was the barking of dogs in the distance. In India the mantras from the temples and the blasting horns of distant trains. Here it's quiet again, finally.

At dusk the moon is already bright and I'm looking forward to camping again. When I'm far away from villages I take a left on a single dirt track. There will be no cars here, which makes the chance of unwanted meetings smaller. The moon is so bright that I barely need a flashlight to put up the tent. I'm in a plantation of teak trees, valuable export products of Myanmar. The trees grow big, dark green leaves. The silence is peaceful and haunting at the same time. No birds, no crickets, no wind—nothing but the soft sound of dew drops dripping from the leaves. When I stand still, I can hear my own heart beating.

The next day people are waving with smiling faces. I stop at a restaurant along the road. It's very basic; there is no electricity during the day. The people are adorably shy. I make eye contact with a young girl who is taking orders. When I say "Hello," she says "Hello" back but then runs back into the kitchen giggling. I have no idea what to order. There is no menu and I don't know the names of the meals or what is available. Normally I take pictures of meals so I can show them as examples later, but this is only the second day in Myanmar and I don't have those pictures yet. My phone is out of service so Google Translate is also not on my side. The people who run the restaurant don't know what I want to eat and we end up lost in translation. In the end, they take me to the kitchen, where I point to some cooking pots, and I'm served some soup, a plate of rice, and some steamed vegetables. I'm good for another 100 kilometers.

→ Myanmar possesses large expanses of tropical forests. Teak hardwood has been an important export product since British colonization (which ended in 1948).

↓ Thanaka, a yellow-white paste, is made from ground up bark. It is part of the culture of Myanmar and usually applied to the faces, and sometimes the arms, of women and children. It protects the skin from sunlight but also functions as make-up.

"I wish I had football shoes. They are cool. But they aren't sold here and I don't have the money for them. I would not wear them but hang them on the wall in my room. I like European football. I really like Arjen Robben. And Mendoza—he plays in India. Tourists never visit my village. I've never talked to someone like you before. I've only seen people like you on TV, so this is a special day for me."

———

Young Burmese man I talked to briefly in a restaurant on the road

Kyauk Ka Latt Pagoda, Hpa-An

291

Entire families, and most often women, working on the roads is a common sight in Myanmar. They frequently live in tents, camping next to the roads, and travel along with the building projects. Fuming tarmac and piles of debris seemed to be handled mainly by female workers.

One of the many roads in Myanmar that is in the process of being paved.

Christmas
At the end of the road

As I get further into Myanmar, the road turns into a total nightmare. The India-Myanmar Friendship Road literally withers away into the land. I ask someone at a crossroads for the best way to Mandalay. There are two roads going southeast from there and I take the more northern route. These choices are always a kind of lottery. Google Maps doesn't say whether a road is paved or not.

There is almost no traffic, apart from the occasional motorcycle or a truck slowly finding its way through the dirt. It doesn't take long until I get stuck in loose sand. It's impossible to continue pedaling while remaining in the saddle. I push the bike for a few hundred meters, until the surface is hard enough to keep the wheels rolling instead of digging them through the dusty, red sand.

The road is actually still being built as I write. Entire families are laboring all day without any modern tools. Even the children are on duty. The men chop big stones into pieces and the women position them on the road with care and precision. An

extremely slow process that continues for about 200 km. In some parts the road consists of big rocks that haven't been crushed yet, and because the landscape is hilly, there is no space next to the road. I end up riding a few hours in the dark, cursing my circumstances. It's almost impossible to keep going. That day I cycle from 9 a.m. till 10.30 p.m. and only make 64 km.

The next day is Christmas but not where I am. All the greenery around me is covered in red dust. It hasn't rained for weeks. I'm a bit hopeless because I have no idea when the road will get better. But after passing a small town my phone has a signal again and there is more traffic. When I take a short break, an SUV passes slowly. I try to look through the blacked out windows but I can't see anything. Probably the exhausted and desperate look on my face makes them stop a couple of hundred meters further up. While I push my bike through the sand, I see an entire family step out and wait for me. A girl, who seems to be the only one who speaks a bit of English, walks up to me and asks if I need help.

I'm saved. Minutes later we're driving over the sandy track with the bike and panniers squeezed in the back. I've been offered the front seat. The ride isn't much more comfortable in the car, but at least it's going faster. After two hours through dirt we're back on tarmac and head for the next city, Monywa. I ask if they can drop me off at a hotel, but when all the hotels turn out to be full, I am offered a bed at their place. It's a very basic house, and it looks like they prepared their best room for me. After I take a shower I offer the old man some whisky from my pannier. We drink together without talking. Christmas arrived unexpectedly.

I had a great night's sleep, and afterwards the roads got better and the real wonders of Myanmar revealed themselves.

← The Laykyun Sekkya Buddha is the third tallest statue in the world, at 116 m high. The fact that it's placed on a 13-meter-tall throne and built on a hill, makes it even more majestic. You can see the gold glitter in the sunlight from miles away. Nearby is a 95-meter-high reclining Buddha (p. 284–85, 299). A lot of Burmese people visit this place as a pilgrimage.

Thanboddhay Pagoda is a Buddhist temple with a huge stupa that looks like Borobudur in Indonesia. It was built in 1303 and reconstructed in 1939. It is said to contain more than 500,000 images of Buddha.

*Each morning
we are born
again. What we
do today is what
matters most.*

Gautama Buddha

Sickness & bike issues

During the first night in Mandalay my stomach decides to do a thorough clear out. Luckily, I'm in a hotel and not on the road, camping somewhere. I probably ate something bad during dinner. It can happen anywhere and anytime, but this is only the second time that I really get sick on this trip.

The first time was in Turkey, when I drank bad water from a river without filtering it. In Turkmenistan I had some minor problems that probably had more to do with the harsh conditions and overall fatigue of making long distances through the hot deserts. I can count myself lucky that I had no troubles at all during two months in India, when I ate street food all the time. However much my stomach got beaten up, it behaved very well, but now it's had enough. I'm grounded for a few days until I get stronger. In the hotel I find a scale and the pointer says 69 kg, which is 11 kg lighter than when I left home nine months ago. I'm back at the same weight as when I was 20 years old.

The downtime gives me an opportunity to clean the bike and do some maintenance. Meanwhile, Nils, who I met on the road in Bulgaria, has arrived in Mandalay. We met a couple of times on the road in Turkey and Central Asia while cycling different routes. He's also grounded, but because the rim of his back wheel got damaged on the train in India. Since then, he had been taking public transport to get to Myanmar. A new wheel is in the mail from Yangon, Myanmar's biggest city. I also have some issues with my bike. During an attempt to fine-tune the gearing I spot that the outer part of the cable seems to be totally ruined. I don't have a spare one. At a mechanic I find a substitute for the outer cable and Nils has a spare inner cable so I'm saved. It would be a challenge to find specific gear like this in Myanmar. Then, some moments later, out of sheer misery, the bolt on my stand breaks. It already got bent by the heavy weight of the load. Without much trouble I find another bolt at a mechanic's shop.

After five days I leave Mandalay. I haven't seen much of the city, other than two hotel rooms. I didn't feel like sightseeing at all; I had seen and experienced so much the past few days that I needed time to lock myself up and reset my brain.

12455 KM MANDALAY

Magic in Bagan

DAY 185 - 12627 KM

The first time I saw images of Bagan was when I watched *Samsara*, a movie depicting the repeated cycle of birth, life, and death. It shows scenes from sacred grounds, disaster zones, industrial complexes, and natural wonders from all over the world, including the plains of Bagan during sunrise. Watching this movie, it never crossed my mind that I would one day arrive here by bike.

An ancient city in the middle of Myanmar, Bagan houses the remains of a wealthy kingdom that once contained 13,000 temples and sanctuaries. Over 2,200 temples and pagodas survive to the present day.

Sleeping under a 1,000-year-old temple

Nils joined me a day later, after his new wheel had arrived in Mandalay. Our plan was to camp in the fields among the temples then get up early and climb one of the temples before sunrise. That's the moment when magic happens in the sky. A wondrous show of nature where the silhouettes of the ancient temples are slowly unveiled in the orange light. The area turns into a fairytale landscape when dozens of hot air balloons lift off and drift over the misty plains. The first day we set up camp next to a temple that was crowded with tourists at sunset. Once it got dark though, we had the place to ourselves. We knew the more rewarding view would be at sunrise, early in the morning, when most tourists are still in their hotel beds.

We had a lot of stories to share from the road. The camp was perfect. A starry night, pleasant temperatures. Nils had invented a new way of making a campfire: putting a yellow stuff sack over a big bottle of water that was lit from the ground by a flashlight. There was no wood to make a real fire and we didn't want to aggravate the authorities. It's amazing to think how much freedom we had camping among these historical architectural wonders. No fences, no guards, no officials. We could spend the night at the most beautiful temples without being disturbed. Something that will definitely change over the next few years as tourism expands.

Early rise

The alarm was set to 5 a.m. I slept lightly so I have no trouble getting up so early.
I cook some rice porridge while Nils is still in his bivvy bag. Rice porridge has been
my main breakfast since Kyrgyzstan. Cooked with milk, ginger, sugar, salt, and some
bananas or other fruits. Nutritious and easy to make. A thermos of coffee gets prepared,
and we are ready to climb the old bricks. We settle down on one of the stairs on the upper
part of the old stone temple. It's chilly, but the porridge and coffee warm us up. Now we
just wait for the light to come. There is excitement in watching the day arrive, especially
when the sun rises so fast as we're close to the Equator. I've seen many beautiful sunrises
during this trip. It's the best start to the day. Darkness to light. Cold to warm. Black to
color. A special moment, alone or shared, while most people are still asleep. Bagan leaves
another jewel in my memories.

Wild camping in Myanmar

P itching our tents in the wild was something we enjoyed a lot after India, where it was a challenge to find a camp spot without being noticed. Nils was responsible for dinner; I took care of breakfast. We were totally done with the countless instant noodles we'd had during this trip, so we went for full cuisine in the field. It wasn't easy to find fresh ingredients in the countryside in Myanmar. There are no supermarkets, only small stores and local markets where most people don't speak a word of English. I googled images of rice, lentils, vegetables, and herbs on my phone to communicate our needs. At other times there were always some strange ingredients we'd never seen before to try in our dishes. Nils got crafty, working in a very limited kitchen with only one stove and his small Swiss army knife. Any homemade dish is delicious after a long day of cycling. Following some glasses of local whisky, we zipped ourselves into our canvas houses for a deep, quiet sleep.

Inle Lake

DAY 272 - 12986 KM

There are a lot of hidden secrets on the waters of Inle Lake. While staying in a neighboring town to take a break from cycling, Nils and I hired a local person with a boat to explore the lake area. A tall skiff with a rattling one-cylinder diesel motor which took us to our destinations in no time. In the wooden houses on Inle Lake you will find the oldest range of local arts and crafts of Myanmar.

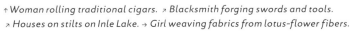

↑ Woman rolling traditional cigars.   ↗ Blacksmith forging swords and tools.
↗ Houses on stilts on Inle Lake. → Girl weaving fabrics from lotus-flower fibers.

Bad roads
The rewards of the unbeaten paths

I enjoy cycling in the dark, when temperatures are more pleasant and everything is quiet. Nils had left our guest-house at Inle Lake earlier that morning. We'd agreed that we would camp together and that I would cycle on in the evening to catch up with him. My ride became slow and unpleasant. The road quality was poor, similar to the first days in Myanmar. I tried to paddle through loose surfaces and attempted to avoid big rocks. It went very slowly. I tried to call Nils to learn where he'd set up camp. No connection. It was too remote.

After a while I cycled past this giant tree and thought it would be the perfect place to camp. Normally I don't sleep so close to the road, but I hadn't seen any traffic in an hour so I didn't see any problems. It was such a magical place. The tree was full of life. In the light of my campfire I saw some rats disappearing under a tree root that was maybe 4 m wide. I wondered how many animals lived there. I even saw some bees buzzing around. It was difficult to get to sleep, but crawling out of the tent into the damp morning air was like waking up in heaven. I was reborn and ready for another day of labor. I was happy I had chosen this route instead of the big road. It was worth the struggle.

The next day Nils and I met again by accident. He'd got taken off the road by officials because foreigners are not allowed to travel in the province using their own transport, and he was delayed. Little did we know. I'd booked a bus in Loikaw and Nils got back just in time to join me on an insane detour trip of 16 hours through the night, covering only 500 km. Early in the morning we arrived in Yangon. After a coffee at the market we said goodbye. I had to be at the Thai border on time because my visa would expire the next day.

Looking back at my time in Myanmar, it's interesting to think about what I expected from it. With every country I visited for the first time on this trip, there were expectations and hopes. You've built an image based on what you have heard, read, and seen in photos. But in the end I always forgot what I was expecting to find and experienced the moment. I was rewarded with very personal and unique experiences and occasions I could never have imagined or predicted. Of course I'd seen the temples of Bagan in pictures, but I never knew how it would be in real life. And you end up in places like this giant tree. The discoveries are what makes the unknown so exciting and the reason for taking the unbeaten paths more worthwhile. Even more reason to go to places that are not recommended — you could be the first one to do so.

THAILAND

DAY 279 - 13330 KM

Patong, Phuket

I'm back to first-world standards and I feel a bit displaced. Like the adventure stops here because everything is so easy. Since cycling through the Middle East and Central Asia, I've dealt with culture shocks, religious restrictions, bad infrastructure, challenging climates. Every country has its own challenges and surprises, and therein lies the beauty of this journey.

First World

From the border town Mae Sot I'm heading straight to Bang kok for a break—to rest and do some maintenance on the bike. A package from home, containing spare parts, a coffee maker (essential travel gear that got broken), and some other things, is waiting there for me. Later I find out that I could've easily got bicycle parts of the same quality here in Thailand. At the first bike store over the border I buy a new pair of padded cycle shorts. I lost mine in the laundry somewhere in India and have been cycling on a pillow ever since.

For days I'm isolated on the freeways with a tailwind help ing me keep the speed at around 30 km/h. Arms resting on the handlebar, head down, headphones on, and enjoying some new music via Spotify. Streaming music was unavailable for the past six months. The ride is uneventful: a flat freeway straight south. It's hot: 30°C plus. Sometimes even above 40. When I step inside an air-conditioned 7-Eleven I realize how warm it actually is outside. During breaks at gas stations I can't get enough ice-cold soda. It's tempting to get a sugar addiction when you do so much exercise in high temperatures, like I'd done this summer in Turkey and Iran. I do more than 100 km a day. It feels insane. Although I

feel fit and strong, this kind of life can't be healthy. The constant inhalation of exhaust fumes, the continuous daily hardship in a climate my body is not used to. Another six days until I'm in Bangkok.

The roads are well paved. Even off the freeway, all the roads are in excellent condition and the traffic rules are obeyed. This is not the Asian traffic I got used to in Turkey, Iran, and India, where intuition is more important than traffic rules. As a Euro pean, it feels very chaotic and unsafe at first, but when you get used to it, you see that it works. In Asia people are used to having to anticipate unexpected traffic and the possibility of a cow or a flock of sheep suddenly being part of the daily commuting ritual.

Thailand will be an easy ride, without much adventure. Thinking about it, sitting on the side of the freeway eating a bag of fresh strawberries in the orange afterglow, I already miss the challenges of "the wilderness." But as my friend Nils writes in an email: "Those chapters are written before; everything has its order. It's time for pleasures and celebrating memories of the trip—the real paradise beaches are still missing."

Bangkok

I enter Bangkok in the pouring rain. I had expected it to be more grubby and chaotic, but after Tehran and Kolkata I have probably seen the worst on this trip. Bangkok's traffic is more fluid. This time I whistle while I zigzag through the lines of cars on the busy streets. A bicycle in central Bangkok is faster than a car, and despite the rain I enjoy the ride. Wet and dirty, I arrive at a hostel in Silom. The floor of my room is a mess of bags, clothes, camping gear, and new bicycle parts. New tires, inner tubes, a chain, and gear cable. The last major changes were done in Tehran, 8,000 km back, so things are starting to fall apart again and it's time for another "pitstop."

I spend my days relaxing, fixing the bike, shopping, watching movies, and hanging out with my friend Mee. She lives in the neighborhood and works around the clock as a personal trainer and fitness blogger. She has the work ethic of a New Yorker. Life can be hectic in the big cities now I am used to such a slow pace and traveling short distances per day. Bangkok has everything that modern Western cities have but for a few dollars less. We're exploring the new restaurants and bars around Silom. I mainly order from European menus. On the road I have no other choice than local food, which is generally delicious in Thailand. But since this little vacation of mine has already taken ten months, I miss eating good pasta or steak. What I also miss are proper clothes. I've been wearing my pink tank top and Adidas shorts for too long now. The sun has bleached the back of the top a few shades lighter and it has spots of tar on it from newly built roads. Close to my hostel I find a mall with only outlet stores. A lot of fashion brands produce their products in Thailand and what doesn't get exported ends up here —luxury brands for bargain prices. At night we end at the rooftop bar of the Pullman Hotel. In white pants, an ironed shirt, and leather shoes I enjoy a bit of Bangkok's cosmopolitan life, far above the city. The view is colorful and the wine is sweet. While examining the skyline of downtown Bangkok my thoughts drift away. The rough days on the road in Myanmar, the adventures in India, and now the pleasures of exotic Thailand. It makes the Silk Road the ultimate trip from Europe. A journey with many chapters.

Bangkok is the hedonistic hub of Southeast Asia, providing affordable thrills for the flip-flopped backpacker. It lures you in using all the colors of the universe, ready to fool you. Like the meat on a stick sold on the street markets. Keep your eyes open because the most beautiful woman you'll meet could just as well be a man. I was happy to be saved from that. So long, Bangkok.

Paradise

On the road, southbound along the seas of Thailand. This is the first camp spot since Myanmar. It's been just too warm to camp. After a long day of cycling in a tropical climate, all I want is an air-conditioned room and a shower. So it takes some determination to find a place to camp with affordable hotels around almost every corner. But I know that it is always worth it. I "tried" to camp on the beach the day before, but I'd got chased by dogs belonging to local residents and then given up when I passed another hotel.

Camping on the beach is pure bliss. The sound of the waves. The rustle of the palm trees in the wind. The cold sand between your toes at night. I was on the east coast of Thailand, so the sun would rise from the sea. I linger a bit before setting up the tent. It is still warm at 10 p.m. The Hilleberg Akto had been serving me well on this trip. A little house weighing just over 1 kg. I strip off the outer tent to be able to have a little breeze inside. It is too warm otherwise. After a salty shower in the sea I zip myself away for the night. A few hours later the waves, which are getting really close to the tent, wake me up. My alarm goes off at 6.15, just before sunrise. A pink sky and a soft warm breeze await my sleepy face. Again I awake in paradise.

The lively shores of Patong beach.

Fishing boats on the Andaman Sea using green lights to attract fish.

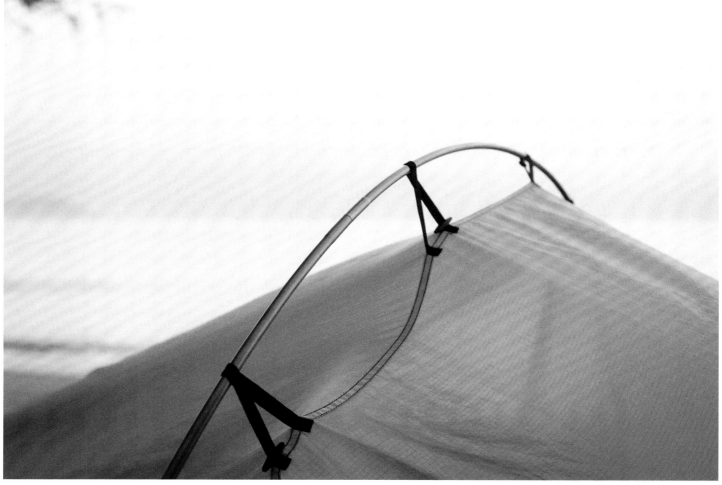

It's 10 p.m., Saturday night, in Krabi, Thailand. Sitting in the sand next to my loaded bike, enjoying a cigarette and the last Chang beer, I wait until the noises around me slowly fade. On the left side is the tourist center of Ao Nang, where the beats echo over the beach. On the right side is a little harbor where fishing boats are preparing to sail out. I am not hiding at all, though I normally would when I spend the night outside. Lights of cars with loud music on pass by and make the shadows of the trees swirl restlessly around me. I wonder if this town ever falls asleep. The air is hot and humid. I have a magnificent view over the green lit sea, framed by palm trees. Limestone islands are towering from the horizon like giant chunks of earth. I crawl into my tent while the sea starts to retreat. Early in the morning I wake up in a different world. When most tourists are still asleep, safely locked in their hotel rooms, I will take the first dive into a virgin sea.

No matter how big the
tourist crowds are in
Thailand, the beach
is always mine in the
morning.

Later, the rituals. Rice porridge with cereal and fresh coffee. I put the stove together and fill up the small one-cup moka pot with coffee from India. While the porridge cooks I take a walk on the empty beach. The sun rises slowly and the first wanderers pass by. They're mostly older people going for a walk. After breakfast I deflate my mattress, pack up the tent, rinse the cooking gear, and load everything on the bike. Now I need to find a boat to take me to the next island.

← *Railay beach.* ↑ *Center: Patong beach.*

Sometimes *I* try to memorize the journey day by day, starting in Amsterdam. For every place *I* spent the night, *I* wrote down one or two keywords in my diary to remember the route *I* cycled. Only the days that *I* stayed longer at one place are faded. But from every day spent on the bike there is something left in my memory.

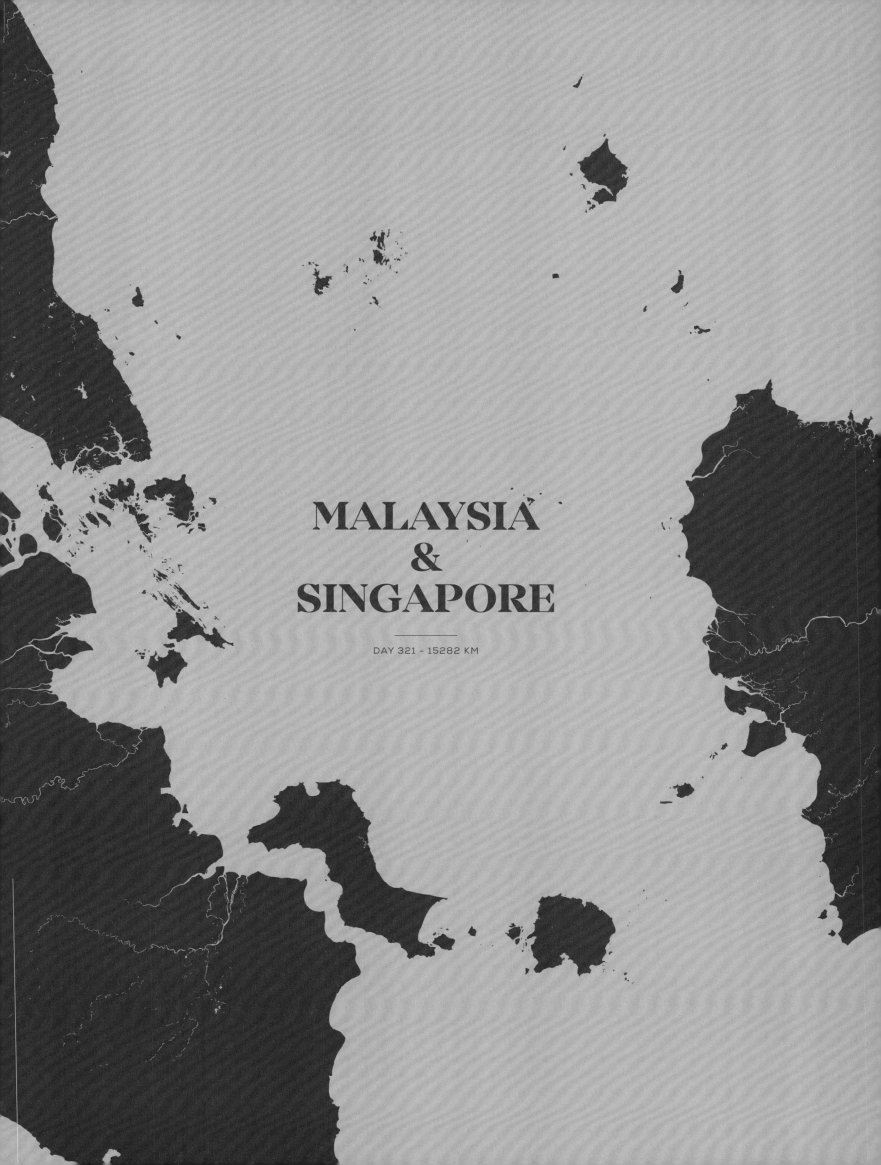

MALAYSIA & SINGAPORE

DAY 321 - 15282 KM

Fighting class

This is Zuhir, 52, a Malaysian Silat fighter who offered to let me stay at his house. I had just crossed the border from Thailand into Malaysia and needed local money to buy food, so I stopped at his restaurant to ask if there was an ATM around. I talked to his son first. He offered me something to eat and drink. I explained I had no money, but it was OK, I got it for free. After he served me some roti canai and fresh sugarcane juice, his father joined us at the table and offered me a bed for three days and food from his restaurant at no cost. I couldn't have wished for a better welcome in Malaysia.

He is a busy man. He has two wives, four sons, five daughters, and 16 grandchildren. He talks all the time. About his classes, the fighting sport, his restaurant, his family. He is a proud and spirited man who wants to give and share instead of making a profit. Young guys from all over the world come and stay at his place to participate in Silat training. It's a niche sport. And it gets even more extraordinary when Zuhir starts to talk about the "sixth sense": practices of pain endurance which are not very common these days. For example, he teaches walking barefoot over burning coals, lying with bare skin on broken glass without bleeding, and keeping a burning coconut on your head without feeling any pain. He showed me old VHS tapes from practices recorded in the 90s. What I saw was intense and I found it hard to believe, but it seemed to be pretty real. He told me these practices are not allowed anymore.

> "We are responsible for everything that lives."

In the evening I joined a fighting class where Zuhir's son was teaching Silat to a group of children. I enjoyed it a lot. Most of the time it looked more like a dancing class than a fighting class. For the children it's a great way to learn discipline, concentration, and motor skills at a very young age. It's hilarious to watch the little boys beating each other up the whole time, as playful as young pups. They were even fighting during the prayer sessions where Zuhir and his sons got together in the big room where we all slept.

At 6 a.m. the alarm went off, signifying another praying session, as happens five times a day. They are dedicated Sunni Muslims. I was happy to see that Muslim women here have a lot more freedom—a contrast to what I had seen in Turkey and Iran, where women are generally more restricted. Here I found a more progressive and tolerant Muslim culture, receiving people with open arms. However, people did have a negative attitude towards Shia Muslims. For example, towards those in Iran, who I mentioned when talking about my travel experiences. I tried to convince Zuhir about the many great people I met in Iran, but the disputes between Shia and Sunnis are deeply rooted.

It's been interesting to learn about religion in all its variet-ies during conversations with people along the way. I have not dedicated myself to any specific religion. I guess I have seen too much and heard too many versions. But religion has saturated every culture. It helps people give structure and meaning to their lives and it adds so much color to the world. Sadly, it also adds a lot of trouble. Once you cling to your own truth too tightly, it's inevitable you will disconnect yourself from others, which for me is a bad thing to begin with. As a Buddhist teacher once told me: "We shouldn't forget we're all connected. We are responsible for every-thing that lives."

Counting down

I'm riding swiftly through Malaysia, making around 100 km a day. It's the very last leg of the journey. I can smell the finish line. Malaysia will probably feel more like a country I passed through instead of visited, with its friendly people living in wonderful houses among the lush, green jungle and bringing me Nasi Goreng and iced coffees. Everything is iced because it's hot, very hot. Temperatures reach around 40°C at midday. The problem with the humid weather is that your sweat doesn't evaporate off your skin and so your body doesn't cool off naturally. Sometimes I can't keep my eyes open because of the sweat pouring into them. I stay in Kuala Lumpur for two days to revel in the pleasure of an air-conditioned condo. I don't explore the city. It's time to finish this journey.

Petronas Towers, Kuala Lumpur

Three kilometers before I reach my goal, I hold still and enjoy the view on Marina Bay. I will miss this life on the road. The freedom, the excitement. Every day a new place, new people, new sights. But I'm also happy that it will end. It has to. I'm tired of adjusting to new environments all the time. I spend more time making a place my own than I do exploring the sights. Also, it takes more to be amazed by something. Traveling can become too much of a routine, and I'm not always seeing the beauty around me. It's good to bring this trip to an end. There will be a lot to look back on. I wonder how long I can sit still and when the itch will come to leave again. Best not to think about it for now.

Fin.
Arrival in Singapore

The last day I cycle the final 70 km to the Gardens by the Bay where Jordy and Monique, Dutch friends living in Singapore, await me. It's a busy route through Johor, a city on the Malaysian side, and then it crosses Singapore from north to south. It goes pretty fast. Before I know it I'm at the border. Everything is neatly organized and I get channeled through the motorcycle lanes. There are hundreds of motorcycles and dozens of immigration booths to process the traffic smoothly. I'm the only one on a bicycle. At the booth I need to fill out a little card and it's a matter of minutes before I'm on the bridge to Singapore.

When I pass the Flower Domes in the gardens I almost collide with a child on a skateboard who is not looking where he is going. This would have been the only accident of this trip,

happening, ironically, in the last 100 m. Luckily, nobody gets harmed. I make a left turn and I see Jordy waving and filming with his phone. There are cheers and smiles. I throw down the bike and hug Monique. I don't know what to say. I'm soaked with sweat and I'm shivering. I forgot to have a proper lunch, so I'm totally out of fuel and feel light-headed. A bottle of champagne is pushed into my hands and I'm fiddling with the cap for a few seconds. Then there's the "pop" and glasses are filled, and slowly I come to my senses. It's only then that I notice the welcome banner they made for me. Sweet people. Such a great welcome. Some more friends and colleagues join us for a drink at Marina Bay. The bike, leaning against a palm tree, is covered in balloons. 17,000 km, 18 countries. From Amsterdam to Singapore by bike. It's done.

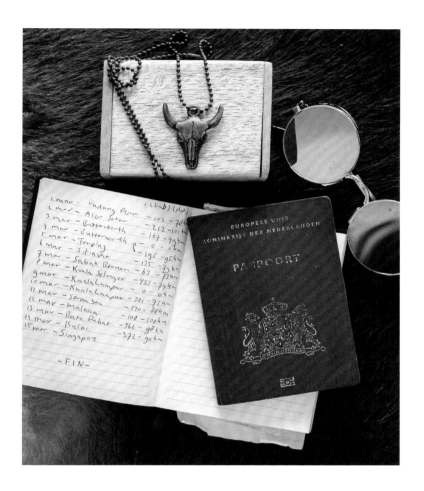

Reunited with family and friends at Schiphol Airport in Amsterdam.

Day 365

Effective distance cycled from Amsterdam to Singapore: 16,032 km

Maximum distance cycled when staying in one location: 1,136 km

Total ascent: 90,417 m

Days on the bike: 212

Maximum speed: 73 km/h (Turkey)

Average speed: 17 km/h

Maximum distance in one day: 154 km (Turkey)

Highest altitude: 3,615 m (Kyrgyzstan)

Lowest altitude: -22 m (Caspian Sea, Iran)

Body weight on departure: 80 kg

Body weight on arrival: 68 kg

Highest bike weight: 62 kg

Number of flat tires: 7

Number of chain changes: 4

Number of tires changed: 2

Number of falls from the bike: 0

Turkey and the Black Sea, as seen from the plane flying back to Amsterdam on April 16th, 2016.

Visas and border crossings

Obtaining visas and border permits can be a lot of hassle on a journey like this, and they require a lot of homework, emails, and embassy visits. Prior to my trip I had nothing prepared, other than passport photos and passport copies. I wanted to travel as freely as possible, planning my itinerary on the go, but once I'd left Europe behind, I needed to plan more carefully as most visas had specific entry and exit dates. On route, I researched online about where I could apply for visas and which border crossings were open and closed. Visa requirements and political situations are changing constantly. The information here is my experience and, therefore, far from complete.

Europe

I crossed Europe without any visas. The first "obstruction" was a small border crossing from Hungary to Romania. As no visa or immigration stamps are needed for Romania, I could've walked around the fence; however, I thought it would be wiser to turn back and cross at an official border. A little detour southward brought me to a crossing at Turnu, where my passport was checked. At the border from Romania to Bulgaria I had to cross the Danube. I was sandwiched between trucks on a narrow bridge. A little scary, but once I'd crossed the bridge I pedaled past the booth without showing any ID.

Turkey

To enter Turkey, you need to purchase a visa for 25 euros, which is available online or at the border. It's valid for three months. I didn't have enough cash on me so I needed to arrange a taxi to take me to a town with an ATM and then return me to the border where I could purchase the visa. This was the first border crossing that didn't go smoothly, but it was my own fault.

Iran

Iran was the first country that required me to obtain a visa upfront. I visited the Iranian embassy in Istanbul, but they told me to contact a travel agency online. I applied at Iranian-visa.com, which cost me about 50 dollars. I could pick up the visa 30 days later in Erzurum, one of the last cities in Turkey on my route. This gave me enough time to cycle there. Other options are Ankara or Trabzon and maybe a few more. The visa procedure was delayed due to Ramadan. Procedures during this religious month in Islamic countries can be unpredict-able and slow because offices might or might not be open for business. It's best to keep pushing by sending emails and to always remain friendly and patient. Once in Erzurum, I had to wait for another week, until the embassy had received the approval letter from Tehran. After handing in my passport and photos I could pick up the visa the next day and I was ready to enter Iran. There are three border crossings into the country. You need to decide upfront where you want to cross. I went to Dogubayazit, which is the most northern crossing, far from the critical areas near Syria and Iraq. There were some military vehicles on the road but it was rather quiet. A month later I heard that there were troubles with the PKK and the border was closed for some time after that. In this case I was lucky.

Turkmenistan and Tajikistan

I stayed for two weeks in Tehran to arrange the visas for Turkmenistan and Uzbekistan. Visas for Central Asia can get very complicated. Luckily I found Caravanistan.com, a convenient website with information about embassy locations, border crossings, opening hours, etc. The visa for Turkmenistan was probably the hardest to obtain. First I needed to get the Uzbek visa because Turkmenistan only gives a five-day transit visa, which you won't get without visas for the countries you exit and enter. I visited the embassy with a pile of documents. Full-color copies of both visas and passport, photos, filled-out application forms you can download online (bring glue to stick your photo on), a motivation letter containing the entry and exit points, dates, and route, and a payment of 70 dollars. The dollar bills needed to be fresh and from a certain year. Old and wrinkled bills are not accepted by banks in Turkemistan. I had brought a pile of cash from Turkey to pay for two months of living and all the visas. Foreigners are not able to withdraw money from ATMs in Iran due to international sanctions. I heard stories of people being refused for a Turkmen visa for no apparent reason. My plan was to pick up the visa after 10 days in Mashhad, a city on my route, not far from the Turkmen border. At the embassy in Tehran they advised me to pick up the visa in Tehran, but I didn't want to wait another seven days. There was a German couple who'd also applied in Tehran. Two weeks later they messaged me saying that their application was turned down without any given reason, so they'd had to book a flight to leave the country. I had heard this story often from travelers so I was lucky. During my last days in Tehran I decided to apply for Tajik visa as well. For this I needed a letter of recommendation from the Dutch embassy, where it was very crowded with Iranian people. As soon as the doorman saw I was Dutch, he let me pass through. Upon arriving at the desk, I learned that the letter would take another week, but after two weeks in Tehran I considered it was time to move on, so I let it go. I reckoned there must be another chance somewhere along the way to apply for the Tajik visa.

The border crossing from Iran to Turkmenistan in Serakhs was slow. Read more about it on page 204.

Uzbekistan

At the Uzbek border I had another long wait. All my bags were checked thoroughly. Photos were shown, my MacBook was examined, and my wallet checked. I filled out a form declaring how much money I was bringing into the country—the last 20 dollars I brought from Turkey. I almost ran out of cash. When I left the country I couldn't take more than that, according to the law. When exiting Uzbekistan two weeks later, things moved along faster. Luckily, because I'd hidden 300 dollars, which I'd withdrawn from the only working ATM in Bukhara, in my shoes.

Kyrgyzstan

At the border of Kyrgyzstan there is less pressure. When driving around in search for the immigration office, I heard a voice: "Come here, handsome!" A middleaged women in official uniform stuck her head out of a window. My passport was stamped and I was in. Kyrgyzstan allows visa-free travel up to 60 days for most passports.

India

I had already decided to go to India by plane. After reviewing the options, it would have been impossible to cycle to India because it requires visas for China and Pakistan, and both were impossible to obtain within a realistic time frame. Once in Osh I took a flight to Bishkek, the Kyrgyz capital, to organize the visas for India and Tajikistan. The last one was high on my list for some time, but luck was not on my side. The Tajik embassy appeared to be closed because they had run out of stickers to apply to passports. At the Indian embassy things worked out better and I could get my visa within two weeks. I flew back to Osh, where my bike still was, and cycled from there to Bishkek.

Immigration at airports always runs a lot smoother because of the number of people traveling by plane. I had a two-month, single entry visa for India. Later it turned out it would've been better to have a double-entry visa so I could cross Bangladesh to skip a lot of distance. There is no open border from Bangladesh to Myanmar so I needed to go all the way around. That's the consequence of not planning the journey ahead.

Myanmar

From India to Myanmar, there is only one border crossing at Moreh/Tamu. This opened to foreigners recently (2014). Apart from a standard visa, you need an extra border permit when you cross over land. The visa I obtained at the embassy in Kolkata took two days to arrange and allowed 28 days in Myanmar. It cost about 20 dollars. For the border permit, I applied at Exoticmyanmartravel.com. This one cost another 80 dollars and it took about 20 days to arrange the permit. The process got delayed and lasted more than a month. I left India on the very last day of my visa.

Thailand

Going overland from Myanmar to Thailand I got a 15-day visa on arrival. I extended it at the embassy in Bangkok. When you apply for a Thai visa outside of Thailand, it's cheaper and you can get up to 60 days.

Malaysia and Singapore

At the Malaysian border I received a stamp in my passport for 90 days, as well as a free bottle of water because I was on a bicycle. Singapore also granted me 90 days, at no cost.

Acquiring visas can be difficult. Doing it yourself instead of through tour agencies can save you a lot of money, but it takes hours of research and it can be stressful too. Sometimes I wished I had planned things further ahead. Tajikistan was a country I really looked forward to but had to skip because I didn't plan my visa application properly. Besides planning, I found out that embassies based in different countries can have totally different rules and policies. Getting a Tajik visa in Kazakhstan is a lot easier than in Iran. Also, rules seem to change all the time according to political situations. Sometimes it's a bit of a lottery, but that all adds to the adventure.

ONE YEAR ON A BIKE

FROM AMSTERDAM TO SINGAPORE

Edited by Martijn Doolaard

Photography, words, and layout by Martijn Doolaard

Editing and proofreading by Tim Mooij-Knip, Lauren Wright, Pascalle van Straten, Lindsey de Leau, and Amy Visram

Illustrations by Rik Wielheesen (pp. 6–7, 94–95)

Maps by Martijn Doolaard and Rik Wielheesen

Special thanks to Stefan van den Heuvel, Tim Mooij-Knip, Milad Torabi, Mirjam Gelink, and everyone who has backed the crowdfunding project on Kickstarter.

Typefaces:
Mirador by Rene Bieder
Nexa by Fontfabric
Baskerville™ by Bitstream
Picadilly by BORUTTA GROUP

Printed by FINIDR s.r.o., Český Těšín

Made in Europe

Published by Gestalten, Berlin 2016
ISBN 978-3-89955-906-4

6th printing, 2023

Who took the photos?
Almost all of the photos in the book were taken by Martijn himself. He uses a Panasonic GH4 camera, which is equipped with a time-lapse function. This means it can be set to take pictures after a set interval, when it's positioned on a tripod. The pictures on pages 84, 260, 270, 278, 318, and 360 were taken by locals or people nearby.

Martijn is a freelance photographer, graphic designer, and filmmaker based in Amsterdam.

*IG: @_espiritu.libre_*
www.espiritu-libre.com

Respect copyrights, encourage creativity!

For more information, and to order books, please visit www.gestalten.com.

Bibliographic information published by the Deutsche Nationalbibliothek.

The Deutsche Nationalbibliothek lists this publication in the Deutsche Nationalbibliografie; detailed bibliographic data are available online at www.dnb.de.

None of the content in this book was published in exchange for payment by commercial parties or designers; Gestalten selected all included work based solely on its artistic merit.

This book was printed on paper certified according to the standards of the FSC®.

MIX
Paper | Supporting responsible forestry
FSC® C014138

Myanmar